PERT Review !

Postsecondary Education Readiness Test Study Guide and Practice Questions

Published by

Blue Butterfly Books™

Published by

Blue Butterfly Books™
Victoria BC Canada

Printed in the USA

Team Members for this publication

Editor: Sheila M. Hynes, MES York, BA (Hons)
Contributor: Dr. C. Gregory
Contributor: Dr. G. A. Stocker DDS
Contributor: D. A. Stocker M. Ed.
Contributor: Brian Stocker MA
Contributor: Elizabeta Petrovic MSc (Mathematics)
Contributor: Kelley O'Malley BA (English)

ISBN-13: 978-0993753770 (Blue Butterfly Books)

ISBN-10: 0993753779

Sustainability and Eco-Responsibility

Here at *Blue Butterfly Books*[TM], trees are valuable to Mother Earth and the health and wellbeing of everyone. Minimizing our ecological footprint and effect on the environment, we choose Create Space, an eco-responsible printing company.

Electronic routing of our books reduces greenhouse gas emissions, worldwide. When a book order is received, the order is filled at the printing location closest to the client. Using environmentally friendly publishing technology, of the Espresso book printing machine, *Blue Butterfly Books*[TM] are printed as they are requested, saving thousands of books, and trees over time. This process offers the stable and viable alternative keeping healthy sustainability of our environment.

All paper is acid-free, and interior paper stock is made from 30% post-consumer waste recycled material. Safe for children, Create Space also verifies the materials used in the print process are all CPSIA-compliant.

By purchasing this *Blue Butterfly Books*[TM], you have supported Full Recovery and Preservation of The Karner Blue Butterfly . Our logo is the Karner Blue Butterfly, Lycaeides melissa samuelis, a rare and beautiful butterfly species whose only flower for propagation is the blue lupin flower. The Karner Butterfly is mostly found in the Great Lakes Region of the U.S.A. Recovery planning is in action, for the return of Karner Blue in Canada led by the National Recovery Strategy. The recovery goals and objectives are aimed at recreating suitable habitats for the butterfly and encourage the growth of blue lupines - the butterfly's natural ideal habitat.

For more info on the Karner Blue Butterfly , feel free to visit:

http://www.albanypinebush.org/conservation/wildlife-management/karner-blue-butterfly-recovery

http://www.wiltonpreserve.org/conservation/karner-blue-butterfly.

http://www.natureconservancy.ca/en/what-we-do/resource-centre/featured-species/karner_blue.html.

Contents

Getting Started

ONGRATULATIONS! By deciding to take the Florida Post Secondary Readiness Test (PERT), you have taken the first step toward a great future! Of course, there is no point in taking this important examination unless you intend to do your very best to earn the highest grade you possibly can. That means getting yourself organized and discovering the best approaches, methods and strategies to master the material. Yes, that will require real effort and dedication on your part but if you are willing to focus your energy and devote the study time necessary, before you know it you will be on you will be opening that letter of acceptance to the school of your dreams!

We know that taking on a new endeavour can be a little scary, and it is easy to feel unsure of where to begin. That's where we come in. This study guide is designed to help you improve your test-taking skills, show you a few tricks of the trade and increase both your competency and confidence.

The PERT Exam

The PERT exam is composed of three main sections, reading, mathematics, and writing. The reading section consists of reading comprehension, analysis of written passages and meaning in context. The mathematics section contains, arithmetic, algebra, geometry and polynomials and quadratic equations. The writing skills section contains questions on sentence structure and rewriting sentences. The writing section contains an essay question, as well as English grammar, spelling, punctuation and usage.

The PERT exam is computer based and adaptive. This means if you answer a questions correctly, the next question will be more difficulty until you reach your level of difficulty. If you answer incorrectly and you are not already at the lowest level of difficulty, the next question will be easier. Each question is multiple-choice, and the exact number of questions varies from student to student depending on how skilled the student is in a particular area.

While we seek to make our guide as comprehensive as possible, note that like all exams, the PERT Exam might be adjusted at some future point. New material might be added, or content that is no longer relevant or applicable might be removed. It is always a good idea to give the materials you receive when you register a careful review.

How this study guide is organized

This study guide is divided into three sections. The first section, self-assessments, which will help you recognize your areas of strength and weaknesses. This will be a boon when it comes to managing your study time most efficiently; there is not much point of focusing on material you have already got firmly under control. Instead, taking the self-assessments will show you where that time could be much better spent. In this area you will begin with a few questions to quickly evaluate your understanding of material that is likely to appear on the PERT. If you do poorly in certain areas, simply work carefully through those sections in the tutorials and then try the self-assessment again.

The second section, Tutorials, offers information in each of the content areas, as well as strategies to help you master that material. The tutorials are not intended to be a complete course, but cover general principles. If you find that you do not understand the tutorials, it is recommended that you seek out additional instruction.

Third, we offer two sets of practice test questions, similar to those on the PERT Exam.

The PERT Study Plan

Now that you have made the decision to take the PERT, it is time to get started. Before you do another thing, you will need to figure out a plan of attack. The very best study tip is to start early! The longer the time period you devote to regular study practice, the more likely you will be to retain the material and be able to access it quickly. If you thought that 1x20 is the same as 2x10, guess what? It really is not, when it comes to study time. Reviewing material for just an hour per day over the course of 20 days is far better than studying for two hours a day for only 10 days. The more often you revisit a particular piece of information, the better you will know it. Not only will your grasp and understanding be better, but your ability to reach into your brain and quickly and efficiently pull out the tidbit you need, will be greatly enhanced as well.

The great Chinese scholar and philosopher Confucius believed that true knowledge could be defined as knowing both what you know and what you do not know. The first step in preparing for the PERT is to assess your strengths and weaknesses. You may already have an idea of what you know and what you do not know, but evaluating yourself using our Self- Assessment modules for each of the three areas, Math, Writing and Reading Comprehension, will clarify the details.

Making a Study Schedule

To make your study time most productive you will need to develop a study plan. The purpose of the plan is to organize all the bits of pieces of information in such a way that you will not feel overwhelmed. Rome was not built in a day, and learning everything you will need to know to pass the PERT is going to take time, too. Arranging the material you need to learn into manageable chunks is the best way to go. Each study session should make you feel as though you have succeeded in accomplishing your goal, and your goal is simply to learn what you planned to learn during that particular session. Try to organize the content in such a way that each study session builds on previous ones. That way, you will retain the information, be better able to access it, and review the previous bits and pieces at the same time.

Self-assessment

The Best Study Tip! The very best study tip is to start early! The longer you study regularly, the more you will retain and 'learn' the material. Studying for 1 hour per day for 20 days is far better than studying for 2 hours for 10 days.

What don't you know?

The first step is to assess your strengths and weaknesses. You may already have an idea of where your weaknesses are, or you can take our Self-assessment modules for each of the areas, Reading Comprehension, Arithmetic, Essay Writing, Algebra and College Level Math.

Exam Component	Rate 1 to 5
Reading Comprehension	
Making Inferences	
Main idea	
Arithmetic	
Decimals Percent and Fractions	
Problem solving (Word Problems)	
Basic Algebra	
Simple Geometry	
Problem Solving	

Essay and English	
Essay Writing	
Basic English Grammar and Usage	
Spelling	
Punctuation	
Capitalization	
Mathematics	
Linear Equations	
Quadratics	
Polynomials	
Coordinate Geometry	

Making a Study Schedule

The key to making a study plan is to divide the material you need to learn into manageable size and learn it, while at the same time reviewing the material that you already know.

Using the table above, any scores of three or below, you need to spend time learning, going over, and practicing this subject area. A score of four means you need to review the material, but you don't have to spend time re-learning. A score of five and you are OK with just an occasional review before the exam.

A score of zero or one means you really do need to work on this and you should allocate the most time and give it the highest priority. Some students prefer a 5-day plan and others a 10-day plan. It also depends on how much time you have until the exam.

Here is an example of a 5-day plan based on an example from the table above:

Main Idea: 1   Study 1 hour everyday – review on last day
Linear Equations: 3   Study 1 hour for 2 days then ½ hour and then review
Algebra: 4   Review every second day

Grammar & Usage: 2 Study 1 hour on the first day – then ½ hour everyday
Reading Comprehension: 5 Review for ½ hour every other day
Geometry: 5 Review for ½ hour every other day

Using this example, geometry and reading comprehension are good and only need occasional review. Algebra is good and needs 'some' review. Linear Equations need a bit of work, grammar and usage needs a lot of work and Main Idea is very weak and need most of time. Based on this, here is a sample study plan:

Day	Subject	Time
Monday		
Study	Main Idea	1 hour
Study	Grammar & Usage	1 hour
½ **hour break**		
Study	Linear Equations	1 hour
Review	Algebra	½ hour
Tuesday		
Study	Main Idea	1 hour
Study	Grammar & Usage	½ hour
½ **hour break**		
Study	Linear Equations	½ hour
Review	Algebra	½ hour
Review	Geometry	½ hour
Wednesday		
Study	Main Idea	1 hour
Study	Grammar & Usage	½ hour
½ **hour break**		
Study	Linear Equations	½ hour
Review	Geometry	½ hour
Thursday		
Study	Main Idea	½ hour
Study	Grammar & Usage	½ hour
Review	Linear Equations	½ hour
½ **hour break**		
Review	Geometry	½ hour

Review	Algebra	½ hour
Friday		
Review	Main Idea	½ hour
Review	Grammar & Usage	½ hour
Review	Linear Equations	½ hour
½ hour break		
Review	Algebra	½ hour
Review	Grammar & Usage	½ hour

Using this example, adapt the study plan to your own schedule. This schedule assumes 2 ½ - 3 hours available to study everyday for a 5 day period.

First, write out what you need to study and how much. Next figure out how many days you have before the test. Note, do NOT study on the last day before the test. On the last day before the test, you won't learn anything and will probably only confuse yourself.

Make a table with the days before the test and the number of hours you have available to study each day. We suggest working with 1 hour and ½ hour time slots.

Start filling in the blanks, with the subjects you need to study the most getting the most time and the most regular time slots (i.e. everyday) and the subjects that you know getting the least time (e.g. ½ hour every other day, or every 3rd day).

Tips for making a schedule

Once you make a schedule, stick with it! Make your study sessions reasonable. If you make a study schedule and don't stick with it, you set yourself up for failure. Instead, schedule study sessions that are a bit shorter and set yourself up for success! Make sure your study sessions are do-able. Studying is hard work but after you pass, you can party and take a break!

Schedule breaks. Breaks are just as important as study time. Work out a rotation of studying and breaks that works for you.

Build up study time. If you find it hard to sit still and study for 1 hour straight through, build up to it. Start with 20 minutes, and then take a break. Once you get used to 20-minute study sessions, increase the time to 30 minutes. Gradually work you way up to 1 hour.

40 minutes to 1 hour are optimal. Studying for longer than this is tiring and not productive. Studying for shorter isn't long enough to be productive.

Studying Math. Studying Math is different from studying other subjects because you use a different part of your brain. The best way to study math is to practice everyday. This will train your mind to think in a mathematical way. If you miss a day or days, the mathematical mind-set is gone and you have to start all over again to build it up.

Study and practice math everyday for at least 5 days before the exam.

Reading Comprehension

THIS SECTION CONTAINS A SELF-ASSESSMENT AND READING TUTORIAL. The tutorials are designed to familiarize general principles and the self-assessment contains general questions similar to the reading questions likely to be on the PERT, but are not intended to be identical to the exam questions. The tutorials are not designed to be a complete reading course, and it is assumed that students have some familiarity with reading comprehension questions. If you do not understand parts of the tutorial, or find the tutorial difficult, it is recommended that you seek out additional instruction.

Tour of the PERT Reading Comprehension Content

Below is a more detailed list of the types of reading comprehension questions that generally appear on the PERT. Make sure you understand all of these points at a very minimum.

- Draw logical conclusions

- Identify the main idea

- Identify secondary ideas

- Identify the author's intent

- Summarizing

- Identify tone

- Distinguish between fact and opinion

The questions below are not the same as you will find on the PERT - that would be too easy! And nobody knows what the questions will be and they change all the time. Mostly the changes consist of substituting new questions for old, but the changes can be new question formats or styles, changes to the number of questions in each section, changes to the time limits for each section and combining sections. Below are general reading questions that cover the same areas as the PERT. While the format and exact wording of the questions may differ slightly, and change from year to year, if you can answer the questions below, you will have no problem with the reading section of the PERT.

Reading Comprehension Self-Assessment

The purpose of the self-assessment is:

- Identify your strengths and weaknesses.

- Develop your personalized study plan (above)

- Get accustomed to the PERT format

- Extra practice – the self-assessments are almost a full 3rd practice test!

- Provide a baseline score for preparing your study schedule.

Since this is a Self-assessment, and depending on how confident you are with Reading Comprehension, timing is optional. A general rule is one minute per question, so allow 25 minutes to complete this self-assessment. Once complete, use the table below to assess your understanding of the content, and prepare your study schedule described in chapter 1.

80% - 100%	Excellent – you have mastered the content
60 – 79%	Good. You have a working knowledge. Even though you can just pass this section, you may want to review the tutorials and do some extra practice to see if you can improve your mark.
40% - 59%	Below Average. You do not understand the reading comprehension problems. Review the tutorials , and retake this quiz again in a few days, before proceeding to the practice test questions.
Less than 40%	Poor. You have a very limited understanding of the reading comprehension problems. Please review the tutorials , and retake this quiz again in a few days, before proceeding to the practice test questions.

Reading Self-Assessment Answer Sheet

1. Ⓐ Ⓑ Ⓒ Ⓓ   11. Ⓐ Ⓑ Ⓒ Ⓓ   21. Ⓐ Ⓑ Ⓒ Ⓓ

2. Ⓐ Ⓑ Ⓒ Ⓓ   12. Ⓐ Ⓑ Ⓒ Ⓓ   22. Ⓐ Ⓑ Ⓒ Ⓓ

3. Ⓐ Ⓑ Ⓒ Ⓓ   13. Ⓐ Ⓑ Ⓒ Ⓓ   23. Ⓐ Ⓑ Ⓒ Ⓓ

4. Ⓐ Ⓑ Ⓒ Ⓓ   14. Ⓐ Ⓑ Ⓒ Ⓓ   24. Ⓐ Ⓑ Ⓒ Ⓓ

5. Ⓐ Ⓑ Ⓒ Ⓓ   15. Ⓐ Ⓑ Ⓒ Ⓓ   25. Ⓐ Ⓑ Ⓒ Ⓓ

6. Ⓐ Ⓑ Ⓒ Ⓓ   16. Ⓐ Ⓑ Ⓒ Ⓓ

7. Ⓐ Ⓑ Ⓒ Ⓓ   17. Ⓐ Ⓑ Ⓒ Ⓓ

8. Ⓐ Ⓑ Ⓒ Ⓓ   18. Ⓐ Ⓑ Ⓒ Ⓓ

9. Ⓐ Ⓑ Ⓒ Ⓓ   19. Ⓐ Ⓑ Ⓒ Ⓓ

10. Ⓐ Ⓑ Ⓒ Ⓓ   20. Ⓐ Ⓑ Ⓒ Ⓓ

Questions 1 – 4 refer to the following passage.

Passage 1 - The Immune System

An immune system is a system of biological structures and processes that protects against disease by identifying and killing pathogens and other threats. The immune system can detect a wide variety of agents, from viruses to parasitic worms, and distinguish them from the organism's own healthy cells and tissues. Detection is complicated as pathogens evolve rapidly to avoid the immune system defences, and successfully infect their hosts.

The human immune system consists of many types of proteins, cells, organs, and tissues, which interact in an elaborate and dynamic network. As part of this more complex immune response, the human immune system adapts over time to recognize specific pathogens more efficiently. This adaptation process is called "adaptive immunity" or "acquired immunity" and creates immunological memory. Immunological memory created from a primary response to a specific pathogen, provides an enhanced response to future encounters with that same pathogen. This process of acquired immunity is the basis of vaccination. [1]

1. What can we infer from the first paragraph in this passage?

a. When a person's body fights off the flu, this is the immune system in action

b. When a person's immune system functions correctly, they avoid all sicknesses and injuries

c. When a person's immune system is weak, a person will likely get a terminal disease

d. When a person's body fights off a cold, this is the circulatory system in action

2. The immune system's primary function is to:

a. Strengthen the bones

b. Protect against disease

c. Improve respiration

d. Improve circulation

3. Based on the passage, what can we say about evolution's role in the immune system?

a. Evolution of the immune system is an important factor in the immune system's efficiency

b. Evolution causes a person to die, thus killing the pathogen

c. Evolution plays no known role in immunity

d. The least evolved earth species have better immunity

4. Which sentence below, taken from the passage, tell us the main idea of the passage?

a. The human immune system consists of many types of proteins, cells, organs, and tissues, which interact in an elaborate and dynamic network.

b. An immune system is a system of biological structures and processes that protects against disease by identifying and killing pathogens and other threats.

c. The immune system can detect a wide variety of agents, from viruses to parasitic worms, and distinguish them from the organism's own healthy cells and tissues.

d. None of these express the main idea.

Questions 5 - 8 refer to the following passage.

Passage 2 - White Blood Cells

White blood cells (WBCs), or leukocytes (also spelled "leucocytes"), are cells of the immune system that defend the body against both infectious disease and foreign material. Five different and diverse types of leukocytes exist, but they are all produced and derived from a powerful cell in the bone marrow known as a hematopoietic stem cell. Leukocytes are found throughout the body, including the blood and lymphatic system.

The number of WBCs in the blood is often an indicator of disease. There are normally between 4×10^9 and 1.1×10^{10} white blood cells in a liter of blood, making up about 1% of blood in a healthy adult. The physical properties of white blood cells, such as volume, conductivity, and granularity, changes due to the presence of immature cells, or malignant cells.

The name white blood cell derives from the fact that after processing a blood sample in a centrifuge, the white cells are typically a thin, white layer of nucleated cells. The scientific term leukocyte directly reflects this description, derived from Greek leukos (white), and kytos (cell). [2]

5. What can we infer from the first paragraph in this selection?

a. Red blood cells are not as important as white blood cells

b. White blood cells are the culprits in most infectious diseases

c. White blood cells are essential to fight off infectious diseases

d. Red blood cells are essential to fight off infectious diseases

6. What can we say about the number of white blood cells in a liter of blood?

a. They make up about 1% of a healthy adult's blood

b. There are 10^{10} WBCs in a healthy adult's blood

c. The number varies according to age

d. They are a thin white layer of nucleated cells

7. What is a more scientific term for "white blood cell?"

a. Red blood cell

b. Anthrocyte

c. Leukocyte

d. Leukemia

8. Can the number of leukocytes indicate cancer?

a. Yes, the white blood cell count can indicate disease.

b. No, the white blood cell count is not a reliable indicator.

c. Disease may indicate a high white blood cell count.

d. None of the choices are correct.

Questions 9 – 12 refer to the following passage.

Keeping Tropical Fish

Keeping tropical fish at home or in your office used to be very popular. Today, interest has declined, but it remains as rewarding and relaxing a hobby as ever. Ask any tropical fish hobbyist, and you will hear how soothing and relaxing watching colorful fish live their lives in the aquarium. If you are considering keeping tropical fish as pets, here is a list of the basic equipment you will need.

A filter is essential for keeping your aquarium clean and your fish alive and healthy. There are different types and sizes of filters and the right size for you depends on the size of the aquarium and the level of stocking. Generally, you need a filter with a 3 to 5 times turn over rate per hour. This means that the water in the tank should go through the filter about 3 to 5 times per hour.

Most tropical fish do well in water temperatures ranging between 24^0 C and 26^0 C, though each has its own ideal water temperature. A heater with a thermostat is necessary to regulate the water temperature. Some heaters are submersible and others are not, so check carefully before you buy.

Lights are also necessary, and come in a large variety of types, strengths and sizes. A light source is necessary for plants in the tank to photosynthesize and give the tank a more attractive appearance. Even if you plan to use plastic plants, the fish still require light, although here you can use a lower strength light source.

A hood is necessary to keep dust, dirt and unwanted materials out of the tank. Sometimes the hood can also help prevent evaporation. Another requirement is aquarium gravel. This will improve the aesthetics of the aquarium and is necessary if you plan to have real plants.

9. What is the general tone of this article?

  a. Formal

  b. Informal

  c. Technical

  d. Opinion

10. Which of the following can not be inferred?

  a. Gravel is good for aquarium plants.

  b. Fewer people have aquariums in their office than at home.

  c. The larger the tank, the larger the filter required.

  d. None of the above.

11. What evidence does the author provide to support their claim that aquarium lights are necessary?

    a. Plants require light.

    b. Fish and plants require light.

    c. The author does not provide evidence for this statement.

    d. Aquarium lights make the aquarium more attractive.

12. Which of the following is an opinion?

    a. Filter with a 3 to 5 times turn over rate per hour are required.

    b. Aquarium gravel improves the aesthetics of the aquarium.

    c. An aquarium hood keeps dust, dirt and unwanted materials out of the tank.

    d. Each type of tropical fish has its own ideal water temperature.

Questions 13 – 14 refer to the following passage.

Vice President Johnson, Mr. Speaker, Mr. Chief Justice, President Eisenhower, Vice President Nixon, President Truman, reverend clergy, fellow citizens:

We observe today not a victory of party, but a celebration of freedom -- symbolizing an end, as well as a beginning -- signifying renewal, as well as change. For I have sworn before you and Almighty God the same solemn oath our forebears prescribed nearly a century and three-quarters ago.

The world is very different now. For man holds in his mortal hands the power to abolish all forms of human poverty and all forms of human life. And yet the same revolutionary beliefs for which our forebears fought are still at issue around the globe -- the belief that the rights of man come not from the generosity of the state, but from the hand of God.

We dare not forget today that we are the heirs of that first revolution. Let the word go forth from this time and place, to friend and foe alike, that the torch has been passed to a new generation of Americans -- born in this century, tempered by war, disciplined by a hard and bitter peace, proud of our ancient heritage, and unwilling to witness or permit the slow undoing of those human rights to which this nation has always been committed, and to which we are committed today at home and around the world.

Let every nation know, whether it wishes us well or ill, that we shall pay any price, bear any burden, meet any hardship, support any friend, oppose any foe, to assure the survival and the success of liberty.

This much we pledge -- and more.

John F. Kennedy Inaugural Address 20 January 1961

13. What is the tone of this speech?

    a. Triumphant

    b. Optimistic

    c. Threatening

    d. Gloating

14. Which of the following is an opinion?

    a. The world is very different now.

    b. For man holds in his mortal hands the power to abolish all forms of human poverty and all forms of human life.

    c. We dare not forget today that we are the heirs of that first revolution

    d. For I have sworn before you and Almighty God the same solemn oath our forebears prescribed nearly a century and three-quarters ago.

Questions 15 – 18 refer to the following passage.

If You Have Allergies, You're Not Alone

People who experience allergies might joke that their immune systems have let them down or are seriously lacking. Truthfully though, people who experience allergic reactions or allergy symptoms during certain times of the year have heightened immune systems that are, "better" than those of people who have perfectly healthy but less militant immune systems.

Still, when a person has an allergic reaction, they are having an adverse reaction to a substance that is considered normal to most people. Mild allergic reactions usually have symptoms like itching, runny nose, red eyes, or bumps or discoloration of the skin. More serious allergic reactions, such as those to animal and insect poisons or certain foods, may result in the closing of the throat, swelling of the eyes, low blood pressure, inability to breath, and can even be fatal.

Different treatments help different allergies, and which one a person uses depends on the nature and severity of the allergy. It is recommended to patients with severe allergies to take extra precautions, such as carrying an EpiPen, which treats anaphylactic shock and may prevent death, always in order for the remedy to be readily available and more effective. When an allergy is not so severe, treatments may be used just relieve a person of uncomfortable symptoms. Over the counter allergy medicines treat milder symptoms, and can be bought at any grocery store and used in moderation to help people with allergies live normally.

There are many tests available to assess whether a person has allergies or what they may be allergic to, and advances in these tests and the medicine used to treat patients continues to improve. Despite this fact, allergies still affect many people throughout the year or even every day. Medicines used to treat allergies have side effects of their own, and it is difficult to bring the body into balance with the use of medicine. Regardless, many of those who live with allergies are grateful for what is available and find it useful in maintaining their lifestyles.

15. According to this passage, it can be understood that the word "militant" belongs in a group with the words:

    a. a. sickly, ailing, faint

    b. b. strength, power, vigor

    c. c. active, fighting, warring

    d. d. worn, tired, breaking down

16. The author says that "medicines used to treat allergies have side effects of their own" to

    a. point out that doctors aren't very good at diagnosing and treating allergies

    b. argue that because of the large number of people with allergies, a cure will never be found

    c. explain that allergy medicines aren't cures and some compromise must be made

    d. argue that more wholesome remedies should be researched and medicines banned

17. It can be inferred that _____ recommend that some people with allergies carry medicine with them.

    a. the author

    b. doctors

    c. the makers of EpiPen

    d. people with allergies

18. The author has written this passage to

    a. inform readers on symptoms of allergies so people with allergies can get help

    b. persuade readers to be proud of having allergies

    c. inform readers on different remedies so people with allergies receive the right help

    d. describe different types of allergies, their symptoms, and their remedies

Questions 19 – 22 refer to the following passage.

When a Poet Longs to Mourn, He Writes an Elegy

Poems are an expressive, especially emotional, form of writing. They have been present in literature virtually from the time civilizations invented the written word. Poets often portrayed as moody, secluded, and even troubled, but this is because poets are introspective and feel deeply about the current events and cultural norms they are surrounded with. Poets often produce the most telling literature, giving insight into the society and mindset they come from. This can be done in many forms.

The oldest types of poems often include many stanzas, may or may not rhyme, and are more about telling a story than experimenting with language or words. The most common types of ancient poetry are epics, which are usually extremely long stories that follow a hero through his journey, or ellegies, which are often solemn in tone and used to mourn or lament something or someone. The Mesopotamians are often said to have invented the written word, and their literature is among the oldest in the world, including the epic poem titled "Epic of Gilgamesh." Similar in style and length to "Gilgamesh" is "Beowulf," an ellegy poem written in Old English and set in Scandinavia. These poems are often used by professors as the earliest examples of literature.

The importance of poetry was revived in the Renaissance. At this time, Europeans discovered the style and beauty of ancient Greek arts, and poetry was among those. Shakespeare is the most well-known poet of the time, and he used poetry not only to write poems but also to write plays for the theater. The most popular forms of poetry during the Renaissance included villanelles, sonnets, as well as the epic. Poets during this time focused on style and form, and developed very specific rules and outlines for how an exceptional poem should be written.

As often happens in the arts, modern poets have rejected the constricting rules of Renaissance poets, and free form poems are much more popular. Some modern poems would read just like stories if they weren't arranged into lines and stanzas. It is difficult to tell which poems and poets will be the most important, because works of art often become more famous in hindsight, after the poet has died and society can look at itself without being in the moment. Modern poetry continues to develop, and will no doubt continue to change as values, thought, and writing continue to change.

Poems can be among the most enlightening and uplifting texts for a person to read if they are looking to connect with the past, connect with other people, or try to gain an understanding of what is happening in their time.

19. In summary, the author has written this passage

    a. as a foreword that will introduce a poem in a book or magazine

    b. because she loves poetry and wants more people to like it

    c. to give a brief history of poems

    d. to convince students to write poems

20. The author organizes the paragraphs mainly by

    a. moving chronologically, explaining which types of poetry were common in that time

    b. talking about new types of poems each paragraph and explaining them a little

    c. focusing on one poet or group of people and the poems they wrote

    d. explaining older types of poetry so she can talk about modern poetry

21. The author's claim that poetry has been around "virtually from the time civilizations invented the written word" is supported by the detail that

a. Beowulf is written in Old English, which is not really in use any longer

b. epic poems told stories about heroes

c. the Renaissance poets tried to copy Greek poets

d. the Mesopotamians are credited with both inventing the word and writing "Epic of Gilgamesh"

22. According to the passage, it can be understood that the word "telling" means

a. speaking

b. significant

c. soothing

d. wordy

Questions 23 – 25 refer to the following passage.

Winged Victory of Samothrace: the Statue of the Gods

Students who read about the "Winged Victory of Samothrace" probably won't be able to picture what this statue looks like. However, almost anyone who knows a little about statues will recognize it when they see it: it is the statue of a winged woman who does not have arms or a head. Even the most famous pieces of art may be recognized by sight but not by name.

This iconic statue is of the Greek goddess Nike, who represented victory and was called Victoria by the Romans. The statue is sometimes called the "Nike of Samothrace". She was often displayed in Greek art as driving a chariot, and her speed or efficiency with the chariot may be what her wings symbolize. It is said that the statue was created around 200 BCE to celebrate a battle that was won at sea. Archaeologists and art historians believe the statue may have originally been part of a temple or other building, even one of the most important temples, Megaloi Theoi, just as many statues were used during that time.

"Winged Victory" does indeed appear to have had arms and a head when it was originally created, and it is unclear why they were removed or lost. Indeed, they have never been discovered, even with all the excavation that has taken place. Many speculate that one of her arms was raised and put to her mouth, as though she was shouting or calling out, which is consistent with the idea of her as a war figure. If the missing pieces were ever to be found, they might give Greek and art historians more of an idea of what Nike represented or how the statue was used.

Learning about pieces of art through details like these can help students remember time frames or locations, as well as learn about the people who occupied them.

23. The author's title says the statue is "of the Gods" because

    a. the statue is very beautiful and even a god would find it beautiful

    b. the statue is of a Greek goddess, and gods were of primary importance to the Greek

    d. Nike lead the gods into war

    d. the statues were used at the temple of the gods and so it belonged to them

24. The third paragraph states that

    a. the statue is related to war and was probably broken apart by foreign soldiers

    b. the arms and head of the statue cannot be found because all the excavation has taken place

    c. speculations have been made about what the entire statue looked like and what it symbolized

    d. the statue has no arms or head because the sculptor lost them

25. The author's main purpose in writing this passage is to

a. demonstrate that art and culture are related and one can teach us about the other

b. persuade readers to become archeologists and find the missing pieces of the statue

c. teach readers about the Greek goddess Nike

d. to teach readers the name of a statue they probably recognize

Reading Self-Assessment Answer Key

1. A

The passage does not mention the flu specifically, however we know the flu is a pathogen (a bacterium, virus, or other microorganism that can cause disease). Therefore, we can infer, when a person's body fights off the flu, this is the immune system in action.

2. B

The immune system's primary function is to protect against disease.

3. A

The passage refers to evolution of the immune system being important for efficiency. In paragraph three, there is a discussion of adaptive and acquired immunity, where the immune system "remembers" pathogens.

We can determine, evolution of the immune system is an important factor in the immune system's efficiency.

4. B

The sentence that expresses the main idea of the passage is, "An immune system is a system of biological structures and processes that protects against disease by identifying and killing pathogens and other threats."

5. C

We can infer white blood cells are essential to fight off infectious diseases, from the passage, "cells of the immune system that defend the body against both infectious disease and foreign material."

6. A

We can say the number of white blood cells in a liter of blood make up about 1% of a healthy adult's blood. This is a fact-based question that is easy and fast to answer. The question asks about a percentage. You can quickly and easily scan the passage for the percent sign, or the word percent and find the answer.

7. C
A more scientific term for "white blood cell" is leukocyte, from the first paragraph, first sentence of the passage.

8. A
The white blood cell count can indicate disease (cancer). We know this from the last sentence of paragraph two, "The physical properties of white blood cells, such as volume, conductivity, and granularity, changes due to the presence of immature cells, or malignant cells."

9. B
The general tone is informal.

10. B
The statement, "Fewer people have aquariums in their office than at home," cannot be inferred from this article.

11. C
The author does not provide evidence for this statement.

12. B
The following statement is an opinion, " Aquarium gravel improves the aesthetics of the aquarium."

13. A
This is a triumphant speech where President Kennedy is celebrating his victory.

14. C
The statement, "We dare not forget today that we are the heirs of that first revolution" is an opinion.

15. C
This question tests the reader's vocabulary skills. The uses of the negatives "but" and "less," especially right next to each other, may confuse readers into answering with choices A or D, which list words that are antonyms to "militant." Readers may also be confused by the comparison of healthy people with what is being described as an overly healthy person--both people are good, but the reader may look for which one is "worse" in the comparison, and therefore stray toward the antonym words. One key to understanding the mean-

ing of "militant" if the reader is unfamiliar with it is to look at the root of the word; readers can then easily associate it with "military" and gain a sense of what the word signifies: defense (especially considered that the immune system defends the body). Choice C is correct over choice B because "militant" is an adjective, just as the words in choice C are, whereas the words in choice B are nouns.

16. C

This question tests the reader's understanding of function within writing. The other choices are details included surrounding the quoted text, and may therefore confuse the reader. A somewhat contradicts what is said earlier in the paragraph, which is that tests and treatments are improving, and probably doctors are along with them, but the paragraph doesn't actually mention doctors, and the subject of the question is the medicine. Choice B may seem correct to readers who aren't careful to understand that, while the author does mention the large number of people affected, the author is touching on the realities of living with allergies rather than about the likelihood of curing all allergies. Similarly, while the author does mention the "balance" of the body, which is easily associated with "wholesome," the author is not really making an argument and especially is not making an extreme statement that allergy medicines should be outlawed. Again, because the article's tone is on living with allergies, choice C is an appropriate choice that fits with the title and content of the text.

17. B

This question tests the reader's inference skills. The text does not state who is doing the recommending, but the use of the "patients," as well as the general context of the passage, lends itself to the logical partner, "doctors," choice B. The author does mention the recommendation but doesn't present it as her own (i.e. "I recommend that"), so choice A may be eliminated. It may seem plausible that people with allergies (choice D) may recommend medicines or products to other people with allergies, but the text does not necessarily support this interaction taking place. Choice C may be selected because the EpiPen is specifically mentioned, but the use of the phrase "such as" when it is introduced is not limiting enough to assume the recommendation is coming from its creators.

18. D

This question tests the reader's global understanding of the text. Choice D includes the main topics of the three body paragraphs, and isn't too focused on a specific aspect or quote from the text, as the other questions are, giving a skewed summary of what the author intended. The reader may be drawn to choice B because of the title of the passage and the use of words like "better," but the message of the passage is larger and more general than this.

19. C

This question tests the reader's summarization skills. The use of the word "actually" in describing what kind of people poets are, as well as other moments like this, may lead readers to selecting choices B or D, but the author is more information than trying to persuade readers. The author gives no indication that she loves poetry (choice B) or that people, students specifically (D), should write poems. Choice A is incorrect because the style and content of this paragraph do not match those of a foreword; forewords usually focus on the history or ideas of a specific poem to introduce it more fully and help it stand out against other poems. The author here focuses on several poems and gives broad statements. Instead, she tells a kind of story about poems, giving three very broad time periods in which to discuss them, thereby giving a brief history of poetry, as choice C states.

20. A

This question tests the reader's summarization skills. Key words in the topic sentences of each of the paragraphs ("oldest," "Renaissance," "modern") should give the reader an idea that the author is moving chronologically. The opening and closing sentence-paragraphs are broad and talk generally. B seems reasonable, but epic poems are mentioned in two paragraphs, eliminating the idea that only new types of poems are used in each paragraph. Choice C is also easily eliminated because the author clearly mentions several different poets, groups of people, and poems. Choice D also seems reasonable, considering that the author does move from older forms of poetry to newer forms, but use of "so (that)" makes this statement false, for the author gives no indication that she is rushing (the paragraphs are about the same size) or that she prefers modern poetry.

21. D

This question tests the reader's attention to detail. The key word is "invented"--it ties together the Mesopotamians, who invented the written word, and the fact that they, as the inventors, also invented and used poetry. The other selections focus on other details mentioned in the passage, such as that the Renaissance's admiration of the Greeks (choice C) and that Beowulf is in Old English (choice A). Choice B may seem like an attractive answer because it is unlike the others and because the idea of heroes seems rooted in ancient and early civilizations.

22. B

This question tests the reader's vocabulary and contextualization skills. "Telling" is not an unusual word, but it may be used here in a way that is not familiar to readers, as an adjective rather than a verb in gerund form. A may seem like the obvious answer to a reader looking for a verb to match the use they are familiar with. If the reader understands that the word is being used as an adjective and that choice A is a ploy, they may opt to select choice D, "wordy," but it does not make sense in context. Choice C can be easily eliminated, and doesn't have any connection to the paragraph or passage. "Significant" (choice B) makes sense contextually, especially relative to the phrase "give insight" used later in the sentence.

23. B

This question tests the reader's summarization skills. Choice A is a very broad statement that may or may not be true, and seems to be in context, but has nothing to do with the passage. The author does mention that the statue was probably used on a temple dedicated to the Greek gods (choice D), but in no way discusses or argues for the gods' attitude toward or claim on these temples or its faucets. Nike does indeed lead the gods into a war (the Titan war), as choice C suggests, but this is not mentioned by the passage and students who know this may be drawn to this answer but have not done a close enough analysis of the text that is actually in the passage. Choice B is appropriately expository, and connects the titular emphasis to the idea that the Greek gods are very important to Greek culture.

24. C

This question tests the reader's summarization skills. The text for choice C is pulled straight from the paragraph, but is not word for word, so it may seem too obvious to be the right answer. The passage does talk about Nike being the goddess of war, as choice A states, but the third paragraph only touches on it and it is an inference that soldiers destroyed the statue, when this question is asking specifically for what the third paragraph actually stated. Choice B is also straight from the text, with a minor but key change: the inclusion of the words "all" and "never" are too limiting and the passage does not suggest that these limits exist. If the reader selects choice D, they are also making an inference that is misguided for this type of question. The paragraph does state that the arms and head are "lost" but does not suggest who lost them.

25. A

This question tests the reader's ability to recognize function in writing. Choice B can be eliminated based on the purpose of the passage, which is expository and not persuasive. The author may or may not feel this way, but the passage does not show evidence of being argumentative for that purpose. Choices C and D are both details found in the text, but neither encompasses the entire message of the passage, which has an overall message of learning about culture from art and making guesses about how the two are related, as suggested by choice A.

Help with Reading Comprehension

At first sight, reading comprehension tests look challenging especially if you are given long essays to answer only two to three questions. While reading, you might notice your attention wandering, or you may feel sleepy. Do not be discouraged because there are various tactics and long range strategies that make comprehending even long, boring essays easier.

Your friends before your foes. It is always best to tackle essays or passages with familiar subjects rather than those with unfamiliar ones. This approach applies the same logic as tackling easy questions before hard ones. Skip passages that do not interest you and leave them for later when there is more time left.

Don't use 'special' reading techniques. This is not the time for speed-reading or anything like that – just plain ordinary reading – not too slow and not too fast.

Read through the entire passage and the questions before you do anything. Many students try reading the questions first and then looking for answers in the passage thinking this approach is more efficient. What these students do not realize is that it is often hard to navigate in unfamiliar roads. If you do not familiarize yourself with the passage first, looking for answers become not only time-consuming but also dangerous because you might miss the context of the answer you are looking for. If you read the questions first you will only confuse yourself and lose valuable time.

Familiarize yourself with reading comprehension questions. If you are familiar with the common types of reading questions, you are able to take note of important parts of the passage, saving time. There are six major kinds of reading questions.

- **Main Idea**- Questions that ask for the central thought or significance of the passage.

• **Specific Details** - Questions that asks for explicitly stated ideas.

• **Drawing Inferences** - Questions that ask for a statement's intended meaning.

• **Tone or Attitude** - Questions that test your ability to sense the emotional state of the author.

• **Context Meaning** – Questions that ask for the meaning of a word depending on the context.

• **Technique** – Questions that ask for the method of organization or the writing style of the author.

Read. Read. Read. The best preparation for reading comprehension tests is always to read, read and read. If you are not used to reading lengthy passages, you will probably lose concentration. Increase your attention span by making a habit out of reading.

Reading Comprehension tests become less daunting when you have trained yourself to read and understand fast. Always remember that it is easier to understand passages you are interested in. Do not read through passages hastily. Make mental notes of ideas that you think might be asked.

Reading Strategy

When facing the reading comprehension section of a standardized test, you need a strategy to be successful. You want to keep several steps in mind:

• **First, make a note of the time and the number of sections**. Time your work accordingly. Typically, four to five minutes per section is sufficient. Second, read the directions for each selection thoroughly before beginning (and listen well to any additional verbal instructions, as they will often clarify obscure or confusing written guidelines). You must know exactly how to do what you're about to do!

• **Now you're ready to begin reading the selection.** Read the passage carefully, noting significant characters or events on a scratch sheet of paper or underlining on the test sheet. Many students find making a basic list in the margins helpful. Quickly jot down or underline one-word summaries of characters, notable happenings, numbers, or key ideas. This will help you better retain information and focus wandering thoughts. Remember, however, that your main goal in doing this is to find the information that answers the questions. Even if you find the passage interesting, remember your goal and work fast but stay on track.

• **Now read the question and all of the choices.** Now you have read the passage, have a general idea of the main ideas, and have marked the important points. Read the question and all of the choices. Never choose an answer without reading them all! Questions are often designed to confuse – stay focussed and clear. Usually the answer choices will focus on one or two facts or inferences from the passage. Keep these clear in your mind.

• **Search for the answer.** With a very general idea of what the different choices are, go back to the passage and scan for the relevant information. Watch for big words, unusual or unique words. These make your job easier as you can scan the text for the particular word.

• **Mark the Answer.** Now you have the key information the question is looking for. Go back to the question, quickly scan the choices and mark the correct one.

Understand and practice the different types of standardized reading comprehension tests. See the list above for the different types. Typically, there will be several questions dealing with facts from the selection, a couple more inference questions dealing with logical consequences of those facts, and periodically an application-oriented question surfaces to force you to make connections with what you already know. Some students prefer to answer the questions as listed, and feel classifying the question and then ordering is wasting precious time. Other students prefer to answer the different types of questions in order of how easy or difficult they are. The choice is yours and do whatever works for you. If you want to try answering in order of difficulty, here is a recommended order, answer fact questions first; they're easily found within the passage. Tackle inference problems next, after re-reading the question(s) as many times as you need to. Application or 'best guess' questions usually take the longest, so save them for last.

Use the practice tests to try out both ways of answering and see what works for you.

For more help with reading comprehension, see Multiple Choice Secrets book at www.multiple choice.ca.

Main Idea and Supporting Details

Identifying the main idea, topic and supporting details in a passage can feel like an overwhelming task. The passages used for standardized tests can be boring and seem difficult - Test writers don't use interesting passages or ones that talk about things most people are familiar with. Despite these obstacles, all passages and paragraphs will have the information you need to answer the questions.

The topic of a passage or paragraph is its subject. It's the general idea and can be summed up in a word or short phrase. On some standardized tests, there is a short description of the passage if it's taken from a longer work. Make sure you read the description as it might state the topic of the passage. If not, read the passage and ask yourself, "Who or what is this about?" For example:

Over the years, school uniforms have been hotly debated. Arguments are made that students have the right to show individuality and express themselves by choosing their own clothes. However, this brings up social and academic issues. Some kids cannot afford to wear the clothes they like and might be bullied by the "better dressed" students. With attention drawn to clothes and the individual, students will lose focus on class work and the reason they are in school. School uniforms should be mandatory.

Ask: What is this paragraph about?

Topic: school uniforms

Once you have the topic, it's easier to find the main idea. The main idea is a specific statement telling what the writer wants you to know about the topic. Writers usually state the main idea as a thesis statement. If you're looking for the main idea of a single paragraph, the main idea is called the topic sentence and will probably be the first or last sentence. If you're looking for the main idea of an entire passage, look for the thesis statement in either the first or last paragraph. The main idea is usually restated in the conclusion. To find the main idea of a passage or paragraph, follow these steps:

1. Find the topic.

2. Ask yourself, "What point is the author trying to make about the topic?"

3. Create your own sentence summarizing the author's point.

4. Look in the text for the sentence closest in meaning to yours.

Look at the example paragraph again. It's already established that the topic of the paragraph is school uniforms. What is the main idea/topic sentence?

Ask: "What point is the author trying to make about school uniforms?"

Summary: Students should wear school uniforms.

Topic sentence: School uniforms should be mandatory.

Main Idea: School uniforms should be mandatory.

Each paragraph offers supporting details to explain the main idea. The details could be facts or reasons, but they will always answer a question about the main idea. What? Where? Why? When? How? How much/many? Look at the example paragraph again. You'll notice that more than one sentence answers a question about the main idea. These are the supporting details.

Main Idea: School uniforms should be mandatory.

Ask: Why? Some kids cannot afford to wear clothes they like and could be bullied by the "better dressed" kids. Supporting Detail

With attention drawn to clothes and the individual, Students will lose focus on class work and the reason they are in school. Supporting Detail

What if the author doesn't state the main idea in a topic sentence? The passage will have an implied main idea. It's not as difficult to find as it might seem. Paragraphs are always organized around ideas. To find an implied main idea, you need to know the topic and then find the relationship between the supporting details. Ask yourself, "What is the point the author is making about the relationship between the details?"

> Cocoa is what makes chocolate good for you. Chocolate comes in many varieties. These delectable flavors include milk chocolate, dark chocolate, semi-sweet, and white chocolate.

Ask: What is this paragraph about?
Topic: Chocolate
Ask: What? Where? Why? When? How? How much/many?

Supporting details: Chocolate is good for you because it is made of cocoa, Chocolate is delicious, Chocolate comes in different delicious flavors

Ask: What is the relationship between the details and what is the author's point?

Main Idea: Chocolate is good because it is healthy and it tastes good.

Testing Tips for Main Idea Questions

1. Skim the questions – not the answer choices - before reading the passage.

2. Questions about main idea might use the words "theme," "generalization," or "purpose."

3. Save questions about the main idea for last. On standardized tests like the SAT, the answers to the rest of the questions can be found in order in the passage.

3. Underline topic sentences in the passage. Most tests allow you to write in your test booklet.

4. Answer the question in your own words before looking at the answer choices. Then match your answer with an answer choice.

5. Cross out incorrect answer choices immediately to prevent confusion.

6. If two of the answer choices mean the same thing but use different words, they are BOTH incorrect.

7. If a question asks about the whole passage, cross out the answer choices that apply only to part of it.

8. If only part of the information is correct, that answer choice is incorrect.

9. An answer choice that is too broad is incorrect. All information needs to be backed up by the passage.

10. Answer choices with extreme wording are usually incorrect.

Drawing Inferences And Conclusions

Drawing inferences and making conclusions happens all the time. In fact, you probably do it every time you read—sometimes without even realizing it! For example, remember the first time you saw the movie "The Lion King." When you meet Scar for the first time, he is trapping a helpless mouse with his sharp claws preparing to eat it. When you see this action you guess that Scar is going to be the bad character in the movie. Nothing appeared to tell you this. No caption came across the bottom of the screen that said "Bad Guy." No red arrow pointed to Scar and said "Evil Lion." No, you made an inference about his character based on the context clue you were given. You do the same thing when you read!

When you draw an inference or make a conclusion you are doing the same thing—you are making an educated guess based on the hints the author gives you. We call these hints "context clues." Scar trapping the innocent mouse is the context clue about Scar's character.

Usually you are making inferences and drawing conclusions the entire time you are reading. Whether you realize it or not, you are constantly making educated guesses based on context clues. Think about a time you were reading a book and something happened that you were expecting to happen. You're not psychic! Actually, you were picking up on the context clues and making inferences about what was going to happen next!

Let's try an easy example. Read the following sentences and answer the questions at the end of the passage.

Shelly really likes to help people. She loves her job because she gets to help people every single day. However, Shelly has to work long hours and she can get called in the middle of the night for emergencies. She wears a white lab coat at work and usually she carries a stethoscope.

What is Shelly's job?

a. Musician

b. Lawyer

c. Doctor

d. Teacher

This probably seemed easy. Drawing inferences isn't always this simple, but it is the same basic principle. How did you know Shelly was a doctor? She helps people, she works long hours, she wears a white lab coat, and she gets called in for emergencies at night. Context Clues! Nowhere in the paragraph did it say Shelly was a doctor, but you were able to draw that conclusion based on the information provided in the paragraph.

There is a catch, though. Remember that when you draw inferences based on reading, you should only use the information given to you by the author. Sometimes it is easy for us to make conclusions based on knowledge that is already in our mind—but that can lead you to drawing an incorrect inference. For example, let's pretend there is a bully at your school named Brent. Now let's say you read a story and the main character's name is Brent. You could NOT infer that the character in the story is a bully just because his name is Brent. You should only use the information given to you by the author to avoid drawing the wrong conclusion.

Let's try another example.

Social media is an extremely popular new form of connecting and communicating over the internet. Since Facebook's original launch in 2004, millions of people have joined in the social media craze. In fact, it is estimated that almost 75% of all internet users aged 18 and older use some form of social media. Facebook started at Harvard University as a way to get students connected. However, it quickly grew into a worldwide phenomenon and today, the founder of Facebook, Mark Zuckerberg has an estimated net worth of 28.5 billion dollars.

Facebook is not the only social media platform, though. Other sites such as Twitter, Instagram, and Snapchat have since been invented and are quickly becoming just as popular! Many social media users actually use more than one type of social media. Furthermore, most social media sites have created mobile apps that allow people to connect via social media virtually anywhere in the world!

What is the most likely reason that other social media sites like Twitter and Instagram were created?

    a. Professors at Harvard University made it a class project.

    b. Facebook was extremely popular and other people thought they could also be successful by designing social media sites.

    c. Facebook was not connecting enough people.

    d. Mark Zuckerberg paid people to invent new social media sites because he wanted lots of competition.

Here, the correct answer is B. Facebook was extremely popular and other people thought they could also be successful by designing social media sites. How do we know this? What are the context clues? Take a look at the first paragraph. What do we know based on this paragraph?

Well, one sentence refers to Facebook's original launch. This suggests that Facebook was one of the first social media sites. In addition, we know that the founder of Facebook has been extremely successful and is worth billions of dollars. From this we can infer that other people wanted to imitate Facebook's idea and become just as successful as Mark Zuckerberg.

Let's go through the other answers. If you chose A, it might be because Facebook started at Harvard University, so you drew the conclusion that all other social media sites were also started at Harvard University. However, there is no mention of class projects, professors, or students designing social media. So there doesn't seem to be enough support for choice A.

If you chose C, you might have been drawing your own conclusions based on outside information. Maybe none of your friends are on Facebook, so you made an inference that Facebook didn't connect enough people, so more sites were invented. Or maybe you think the people who connect on Facebook are too old, so you don't think Facebook connects enough people your age. This might be true, but remember inferences should be drawn from the information the author gives you!

If you chose D, you might be using the information that Mark Zuckerberg is worth over 28 billion dollars. It would be easy for him to pay others to design new sites, but remember, you need to use context clues! He is very wealthy, but that statement was giving you information about how successful Facebook was—not suggesting that he paid others to design more sites!

So remember, drawing inferences and conclusions is simply about using the information you are given to make an educated guess. You do this every single day so don't let this concept scare you. Look for the context clues, make sure they support your claim, and you'll be able to make accurate inferences and conclusions!

Meaning From Context

Often in Reading Comprehension questions, you are asked for the definition of a word, which you have to infer from the surrounding text, called "meaning in context." Here are a few examples with step-by-step solutions, and a few tips and tricks to answering meaning from context questions.

There are thousands of words in the English language. It is impossible for us to know what every single one of them means, but we also don't have time to Google a definition every time we read a word we don't understand! Even the smartest person in the world comes across words they don't know, but luckily we can use context clues to help us determine what things actually mean.

Context clues are really just little hints that can help us determine the meaning of words or phrases and honestly, the easiest way to learn how to use context clues is to practice!

Let's start with a few basic examples.

In some countries many people are not given access to schools, teachers, or books. In these countries, people might be illiterate.

You might not know what the word illiterate means, but let's use the clues in the sentence to help us. If people are not given access to schools, teachers, or books, what might happen? They probably don't learn what we learned in school so they might not know some of the things that we learned from our teachers! Illiterate actually means "unable to read or write." This makes sense based on the context clues!

Let's work through another example.

We have so much technology today! So much technology that many people have started using tablets and computers to read ebooks instead of paper books! In fact, some of these people actually think that reading paper books is archaic!

Let's look for the context clues. Well, what do we know from this paragraph? We have a lot of technology and sometimes people read ebooks instead of paper books. From this we can draw the conclusion that ebooks are beginning to replace paper books because ebooks are newer and better. So if ebooks are newer and better, it must mean that paper books are older. Archaic actually means "very old or old-fashioned," which again we determined from the context clues.

Let's see if you can try a few on your own now.

Cody noticed the strawberries in his refrigerator were old and moldy, so he abstained and threw them away. What does abstained most likely mean?

a. chose not to consume

b. washed

c. shared

d. cut into pieces

The correct answer here is A. The context clues told you the strawberries were old and moldy, and that Cody did something and then threw them away. If the strawberries were moldy, and Cody abstained, it makes sense that he didn't eat them—which is choice A.

You may have chosen choice B. If the strawberries were old and moldy, Cody could have washed them. But use ALL of the context clues. After he abstained, he threw them away. Why would Cody wash them and then throw them away? That doesn't make sense! In addition, why would he share them if they were old and moldy? Finally, I suppose Cody could have cut them into pieces, but why would he need to do that before throwing them away? It doesn't make as much sense, so choice A is the correct answer!

Let's do one more.

Scott had disdain for Lily ever since she lied to their boss and got him fired.

a. Compassion

b. Hate

c. Remorse

d. Money

The correct answer is B. Scott was fired because Lily lied. Can you imagine if this happened to you? I think you would have some pretty strong feelings just like Scott!

By understanding the context, you can determine the meaning of even the hardest of words!

Point Of View And Purpose

You may not think so, but everything you read was written for a purpose. Now, it might not be the most exciting purpose, but regardless of whether it's a website, a magazine article, a book, or even a Facebook status—everything is written for a particular purpose. By understanding that purpose and the author's point of view, we can better comprehend what we read!

To determine the purpose of a written piece, you are asking yourself a very easy question. Why was this written? Usually the answer will be one of these three choices:

1. To inform
2. To persuade
3. To entertain.

First, you should ask yourself if the piece is fiction or non-fiction. Fiction is a type of writing that is not true. It is imaginary, made-up, or theoretical. For example, Harry Potter is fiction. While reading, it may seem like this world of wizards exists, but in reality, there is no Hogwarts or Diagon Alley. It is imaginary. Can you guess which purpose fiction has? Correct, choice 3—to entertain! So if you can tell if a piece is fiction or non-fiction, you can begin to narrow down the author's purpose!

Now, if a piece is non-fiction you are left with choice 1 or 2. To inform or to persuade. Here's another trick. If the piece is simply giving you INFORMation, the author's purpose is most likely to inform you! Think of an example of an informational piece you've read recently. Textbooks, most newspaper articles, how-to blogs, the instruction manual for your new cell phone, all these are great examples where the author's purpose was to inform you.

Some nonfiction pieces, though, are written to persuade you—meaning they are trying to convince you to do something or believe something. Can you think of a few examples where the author's purpose was to persuade?

When an author's purpose is to persuade you, they will have a point of view. What side is the author on? What are they trying to convince you to believe or do? Understanding a point of view will help you better understand the author's purpose.

Let's try a few examples. Determine what the author's purpose is for each of the following:

1. A packet that explains how to use an Xbox One

2. A story where a student plays Xbox One every day and becomes the youngest person to invent an Xbox One game.

3. An article that discusses the dangers of Xbox One and says nobody should ever play.

All three of these examples have similar information—Xbox One. However, the author has a different purpose in each.

Number 1 is simply to inform. It is giving you INFORMation. Number 2 is to entertain. It is a fiction story based on imagination, not facts. Number 3 is to persuade—the author is trying to convince readers that Xbox One is bad and people should stop playing.

Now that we have a better understanding of purpose, let's dive into point of view a little deeper. Read the passage below and answer the questions.

Mac computers are better than PC Computers. Mac computers are more expensive, but they are worth every penny. They are made better than PC computers and typically last longer. They have better software programs and almost never get viruses or break down. PC computers have to get fixed or replaced all the time and it ends up being more expensive than just buying a Mac computer in the first place! Plus, Mac computers are more user friendly and they will sync with your Ipad and Iphone! I highly suggest getting a Mac if you are looking to buy a new computer.

What was the author's purpose when they wrote this paragraph?

a. Inform

b. Persuade

c. Entertain

Right, you should have chosen B, to persuade. The author has an opinion, which suggests they are persuading you to do something.

What is the author's point of view?

a. PC Computers are the best computers to buy

b. Both Mac's and PC's are great computers if you take care of them

c. Mac Computers are better than PC Computers

d. Everybody should own tablets rather than computers

The correct answer is C. The author clearly thinks that Mac computers are better than PC's. This is their point of view, or what side of the argument they are on! By understanding the author's purpose and point of view, you can better understand what you read. Just remember, everything was written for a purpose! Once you understand that purpose, you can better comprehend what point the author is trying to make!

Mathematics

THIS SECTION CONTAINS A SELF-ASSESSMENT AND MATH TUTO-
RIALS. The tutorials are designed to familiarize general principles and the self-assessment contains general questions
similar to the math questions likely to be on the PERT exam,
but are not intended to be identical to the exam questions.
The tutorials are not designed to be a complete math course,
and it is assumed that students have some familiarity with
math. If you do not understand parts of the tutorial, or find
the tutorial difficult, it is recommended that you seek out
additional instruction.

Tour of the PERT Mathematics Content

Below is a list of the likely mathematics topics likely to appear on the PERT. Make sure that you understand these
topics.

Basic Mathematics

- Algebra

- Simple geometry and measurement

- Operations with polynomials

- Solving Inequalities

- Linear equations with one and two variables

- Solving quadratics

- Coordinate geometry

The questions in the self-assessment are not the same as you will find on the PERT - that would be too easy! And nobody knows what the questions will be and they change all the time. Mostly, the changes consist of substituting new questions for old, but the changes also can be new question formats or styles, changes to the number of questions in each section, changes to the time limits for each section, and combining sections. So, while the format and exact wording of the questions may differ slightly, and changes from year to year, if you can answer the questions below, you will have no problem with the mathematics section of the PERT.

Mathematics Self-Assessment

The purpose of the self-assessment is:

- Identify your strengths and weaknesses.

- Develop your personalized study plan (above)

- Get accustomed to the PERT format

- Extra practice – the self-assessments are almost a full 3rd practice test!

- Provide a baseline score for preparing your study schedule.

Since this is a Self-assessment, and depending on how confident you are with mathematics, timing yourself is optional.

Once complete, use the table below to assess your understanding of the content, and prepare your study schedule described in chapter 1.

80% - 100%	Excellent – you have mastered the content
60 – 79%	Good. You have a working knowledge. Even though you can just pass this section, you may want to review the tutorials and do some extra practice to see if you can improve your mark.
40% - 59%	Below Average. You do not understand the content. Review the tutorials , and retake this quiz again in a few days, before proceeding to the practice test questions.
Less than 40%	Poor. You have a very limited understanding. Please review the tutorials , and retake this quiz again in a few days, before proceeding to the practice test questions.

Mathematics Self-Assessment
Answer Sheet

1. Ⓐ Ⓑ Ⓒ Ⓓ   11. Ⓐ Ⓑ Ⓒ Ⓓ

2. Ⓐ Ⓑ Ⓒ Ⓓ   12. Ⓐ Ⓑ Ⓒ Ⓓ

3. Ⓐ Ⓑ Ⓒ Ⓓ   13. Ⓐ Ⓑ Ⓒ Ⓓ

4. Ⓐ Ⓑ Ⓒ Ⓓ   14. Ⓐ Ⓑ Ⓒ Ⓓ

5. Ⓐ Ⓑ Ⓒ Ⓓ   15. Ⓐ Ⓑ Ⓒ Ⓓ

6. Ⓐ Ⓑ Ⓒ Ⓓ   16. Ⓐ Ⓑ Ⓒ Ⓓ

7. Ⓐ Ⓑ Ⓒ Ⓓ   17. Ⓐ Ⓑ Ⓒ Ⓓ

8. Ⓐ Ⓑ Ⓒ Ⓓ   18. Ⓐ Ⓑ Ⓒ Ⓓ

9. Ⓐ Ⓑ Ⓒ Ⓓ   19. Ⓐ Ⓑ Ⓒ Ⓓ

10. Ⓐ Ⓑ Ⓒ Ⓓ   20. Ⓐ Ⓑ Ⓒ Ⓓ

Mathematics Self-Assessment

1. Express in 3^4 standard form

   a. 81

   b. 27

   c. 12

   d. 9

2. Simplify $4^3 + 2^4$

   a. 45

   b. 108

   c. 80

   d. 48

3. If $x = 2$ and $y = 5$, solve $xy^3 - x^3$

   a. 240

   b. 258

   c. 248

   d. 242

4. $X^3 \times X^2 =$

   a. 5^x

   b. x^{-5}

   c. x^{-1}

   d. X^5

5. Express 100000^0 in standard form.

a. 1
b. 0
c. 100000
d. 1000

6. Solve the linear equation: $-x - 7 = -3x - 9$

a. -1
b. 0
c. 1
d. 2

7. Solve the system: $4x - y = 5$ $x + 2y = 8$

a. (3,2)
b. (3,3)
c. (2,3)
d. (2,2)

8. Add $-3x^2 + 2x + 6$ and $-x^2 - x - 1$.

a. $-2x^2 + x + 5$
b. $-4x^2 + x + 5$
c. $-2x^2 + 3x + 5$
d. $-4x^2 + 3x + 5$

9. Simplify the following expression:

$3x^3 + 2x^2 + 5x - 7 + 4x^2 - 5x + 2 - 3x^3$

a. $6x^2 - 9$
b. $6x^2 - 5$
c. $6x^2 - 10x - 5$
d. $6x^2 + 10x - 9$

10. Multiply x - 1 and $x^2 + x + 2$.

    a. $x^3 + x - 2$

    b. $x^2 + x - 2$

    c. $x^3 + x^2 - 2$

    d. $x^3 + 2x^2 - 2$

11. Factor the polynomial $9x^2 - 6x + 12$.

    a. $3(x^2 - 2x + 9)$

    b. $3(3x^2 - 3x + 4)$

    c. $9(x^2 - 3x + 3)$

    d. $3(3x^2 - 2x + 4)$

12. Find 2 numbers that sum to 21 and the sum of the squares is 261.

    a. 14 and 7

    b. 15 and 6

    c. 16 and 5

    d. 17 and 4

13. Using the factoring method, solve the quadratic equation: $x^2 + 4x + 4 = 0$

    a. 0 and 1

    b. 1 and 2

    c. 2

    d. -2

14. Using the quadratic formula, solve the quadratic equation: $x - 31/x = 0$

    a. $-\sqrt{13}$ and $\sqrt{13}$

    b. $-\sqrt{31}$ and $\sqrt{31}$

    c. $-\sqrt{31}$ and $2\sqrt{31}$

    d. $-\sqrt{3}$ and $\sqrt{3}$

15. Using the factoring method, solve the quadratic equation: $2x^2 - 3x = 0$

    a. 0 and 1.5

    b. 1.5 and 2

    c. 2 and 2.5

    d. 0 and 2

16. Using the quadratic formula, solve the quadratic equation: $x^2 - 9x + 14 = 0$

    a. 2 and 7

    b. -2 and 7

    c. -7 and -2

    d. -7 and 2

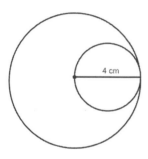

4 cm

17. What is (area of large circle) - (area of small circle) in the figure above?

    a. 8 π cm²

    b. 10 π cm²

    c. 12 π cm²

    d. 16 π cm²

18. What is the length of each side of the indicated square above?

    a. 10
    b. 15
    c. 20
    d. 5

19. Solve the inequality: -7x - 1 ≥ 13

    a. (2, + ∞)

    b. (7, + ∞)

    c. (-∞, -2)

    d. (2, + ∞)

20. Solve the inequality: 2x - 1 ≥ x + 10

    a. (-∞, 9)

    b. (9, +∞)

    c. (-∞, -9)

    d. (11, +∞)

ANSWER KEY

1. A
3 x 3 x 3 x 3 = 81

2. C
(4 x 4 x 4) + (2 x 2 x 2 x 2) = 64 + 16 = 80

3. D
$2(5)^3 - (2)^3$ = 2(125) – 8 = 250 – 8 = 242

4. D
X^3 x X^2 = X^{3+2} = X^5
To multiply exponents with like bases, add the exponents.

5. A
Any value (except 0) raised to the power of 0 equals 1.

6. A
-x - 7 = -3x - 9
-x + 3x = -9 + 7
2x = -2
x = (-2)/2
x = -1

7. C
(2, 3)
4x - y = 5
x + 2y = 8
y = 4x - 5
x + 2(4x - 5) = 8
x + 8x - 10 = 8
x + 8x - 10 = 8
9x = 10 + 8
9x = 18
x = 2

Use solution, x = 2 to find y.

y = (4 * 2) - 5
y = 8 - 5
y = 3

8. B
$-4x^2 + x + 5$

$(-3x^2 + 2x + 6) + (-x^2 - x - 1)$
$-3x^2 + 2x + 6 - x^2 - x - 1$
$-4x^2 + x + 5$

9. B
$6x^2 - 5$

$3x^3 + 2x^2 + 5x - 7 + 4x^2 - 5x + 2 - 3x^3 = 6x^2 - 5$

10. A
$x^3 + x - 2$

$(x - 1)(x^2 + x + 2) = x^3 + x^2 + 2x - x^2 - x - 2 = x^3 + x - 2$

11. D
$3(3x^2 - 2x + 4)$

$9x^2 - 6x + 12 = 3 * 3x^2 - 2 * 3x + 3 * 4 = 3(3x^2 - 2x + 4)$

12. B
The numbers are 15 and 6.
$x + 7 = 21 \Rightarrow x = 21 - 7$
$x^2 + y^2 = 261$

$(21 - 7)^2 + y^2 = 261$
$441 - 42y + y^2 + y^2 = 261$
$2y^2 - 42y + 180 = 0$
$y^2 - 21y + 90 = 0$
$y_{1,2} = 21 \pm \sqrt{441 - 360}/2$
$y_{1,2} = 21 \pm \sqrt{81}/2$
$y_{1,2} = 21 \pm 9/2$
$\mathbf{y_1 = 15}$
$\mathbf{y_2 = 6}$
$x_1 = 21 = y_1 = 21 - 15 = 6$
$x_2 = 21 - y_2 = 21 - 6 = 15$

13. D

-2

$$x^2 + 4x + 4 = 0$$

$$x^2 + 2x + 2x + 4 = 0$$

$$x(x+2) + 2(x+2) = 0$$

$$(x+2)(x+2) = 0$$

$$(x+2)^2 = 0$$

$$x = -2$$

14. B

$-\sqrt{31}$ and $\sqrt{31}$

$$x - \frac{31}{x} = 0$$

$$\frac{x^2 - 31}{x} = 0 \Rightarrow x^2 - 31 = 0$$

$$x_{1,2} = \frac{0 \pm \sqrt{-4 \cdot (-31)}}{2}$$

$$x_{1,2} = \frac{\pm 2\sqrt{31}}{2}$$

$$x_{1,2} = \pm\sqrt{31}$$

$$x_1 = \sqrt{31}$$

$$x_2 = -\sqrt{31}$$

15. A

0 and 1.5

$2x^2 - 3x = 0$

$x(2x - 3)$

x = 0 or 2x - 3 = 0

x = 0 or x = 3/2

x = 0 or x = 1.5

16. A
2 and 7

$$x^2 - 9x + 14 = 0$$

$$x_{1,2} = \frac{-(-9) \pm \sqrt{(-9)^2 - 4 \cdot 14}}{2 \cdot 1}$$

$$x_{1,2} = \frac{9 \pm \sqrt{81 - 56}}{2}$$

$$x_{1,2} = \frac{9 \pm \sqrt{25}}{2}$$

$$x_{1,2} = \frac{9 \pm 5}{2}$$

$$x_1 = \frac{9 + 5}{2} = 7$$

$$x_2 = \frac{9 - 5}{2} = 2$$

17. C

Given: Two circles with a smaller circle (diameter given) exactly half the larger circle (radius given).
Difference = (Area of large circle) - (Area of small large circle)
π 4^2 - π 2^2
= 16π - 4π
Difference = 12π cm^2

18. B
Pythagorean Theorem:
(Hypotenuse)^2 = (Perpendicular)^2 + (Base)^2
$h^2 = a^2 + b^2$

$a^2 = 81$, $b^2 = 144$
$h^2 = a^2 + b^2$
$h^2 = 81 + 144$
$h^2 = 225$
h = 15

19. C (-∞, -2)

-7x - 1 ≥ 13
-7x ≥ 13 + 1

-7x ≥ 14
-x ≥ 2/(-1)
x ≤ -2

20. D
2x - 1 ≥ x + 10
2x - x ≥ 10 + 1
x ≥ 11

Solving One-Variable Linear Equations

Linear equations with variable x is an equation with the following form:

$$ax = b$$

where a and b are real numbers. If a=0 and b is different from 0, then the equation has no solution.

Let's solve one simple example of a linear equation with one variable:

$$4x - 2 = 2x + 6$$

When we are given this type of equation, we are always moving variables to the one side, and real numbers to the other side of the equals sign. Always remember: if you are changing sides, you are changing signs. Let's move all variables to the left, and real number to the right side:

4x - 2 = 2x + 6
4x - 2x = 6 + 2
2x = 8
x = 8/2
x = 4

When 2x goes to the left it becomes -2x, and -2 goes to the right and becomes +2. After calculations, we find that x is 4, which is a solution of our linear equation.

Let's solve a little more complex linear equation:

2x - 6/4 + 4 = x
2x - 6 + 16 = 4x
2x - 4x = -16 + 6
-2x = -10
x = -10/-2
x = 5

We multiply whole equation by 4, to lose the fractional line. Now we have a simple linear equation. If we change sides, we change the signs.

Solving Two-Variable Linear Equations

If we have 2 or more linear equations with 2 or more variables, then we have a system of linear equations. The idea here is to express one variable using the other in one equation, and then use it in the second equation, so we get a linear equation with one variable. Here is an example:

x - y = 3
2x + y = 9

From the first equation, we express y using x.

y = x - 3

In the second equation, we write x-3 instead of y. And there we get a linear equation with one variable x.

2x + x - 3 = 9
3x = 9 + 3
3x = 12
x = 12/3
x = 4

Now that we found x, we can use it to find y.

y = x - 3
y = 4 - 3
y = 1

So, the solution of this system is (x,y) = (4,1).

Let's solve one more system using a different method:

Solve:

5x - 3y = 17
x + 3y = 11

5x - 3y + x + 3y = 17 - 11

Notice that we have -3y in the first equation and +3y in the second. If we add these 2, we get zero, which means we lose variable y. So, we add these 2 equations and we get a linear equation with one variable.

6x = 6
x = 1

Now that we have x, we use it to find y.

5 - 3y = 17
-3y = 17 - 5
-3y = 12
y = 12/(-3)
y = -4

Adding and Subtracting Polynomials

When we are adding or subtracting 2 or more polynomials, we have to first group the same variables (arguments) that have the same degrees and then add or subtract them. For example, if we have ax^3 in one polynomial (where a is some real number), we have to group it with bx^3 from the other polynomial (where b is also some real number). Here is one example with adding polynomials:

$(-x^2 + 2x + 3) + (2x^2 + 4x - 5)=$
$-x^2 + 2x + 3 + 2x^2 + 4x - 5 =$
$x^2 + 6x - 2$

We remove the brackets, and since we have a plus in front of every bracket, the signs in the polynomials don't change. We group variables with the same degrees. We have -1 + 2, which is 1 and that's how we got x^2. For the first degree, where we have 2 + 4 which is 6, and the constants (real numbers) where we have 3 - 5 which is -2.

The principle is the same with subtracting, only we have to keep in mind that a minus in front of the polynomial changes all signs in that polynomial. Here is one example:

$(4x^3 - x^2 + 3) \ominus (-3x^2 - 10) =$
$4x^3 - x^2 + 3 + 3x^2 + 10 =$
$4x^3 + 2x^2 + 13$

We remove the brackets, and since we have a minus in front of the second polynomial, all signs in that polynomial change. We have -3 x 2 and with minus in front, it becomes a plus and same goes for -10.

Now we group the variables with same degrees: there is no variable with the third degree in the second polynomial, so we just write 4 x 3. We group other variables the same way as adding polynomials.

Multiplying and Dividing Polynomials

If we have two polynomials that we need to multiply, then multiply each member of the first polynomial with each member of the second.   Let's see in one example how this works:

$(x-1)(x-2) = x^2 - 2x - x + 2 = x^2 - 3x + 2$

The first member of the first polynomial is multiplied with the first member of the second polynomial and then with the second member of the second polynomial. Continue the process with the second member of the first polynomial, then simplify.

To multiply more polynomials, multiply the first 2, then multiply that result with next polynomial and so on. Here is one example:

$(1 - x)(2 - x)(3 - x) = (2 - x - 2x + x^2) (3-x)$
$= (2 - 3x + x^2) (3 - x)$
$= 6 - 2x - 9x + 3x^2 + 3x^2 - x^3 = 6 - 11x + 6x^2 - x^3$

Simplifying Polynomials

Let's say we are given some expression with one or more variables, where we have to add, subtract and multiply polynomials. We do the calculations with variables and constants and then we group the variables with the appropriate degrees. As a result, we would get a polynomial. This process is called simplifying polynomials, where we go from a complex expression to a simple polynomial.

Example:

Simplify the following expression and arrange the degrees from bigger to smaller:

$4 + 3x - 2x^2 + 5x + 6x^3 - 2x^2 + 1 = 6x^3 - 4x^2 + 8x + 5$

We can have more complex expressions such as:

$(x + 5)(1 - x) - (2x - 2) = x - x^2 + 5 - 5x - 2x + 2 = -x^2 - 6x + 7$

Here, first we multiply the polynomials and then we subtract the result and the third polynomial.

Factoring Polynomials

If we have a polynomial that we want to write as multiplication of a real number and a polynomial or as a multiplication of 2 or more polynomials, then we are dealing with factoring polynomials.

Let's see an example for a simple factoring:

$12x^2 + 6x - 4 =$
$2 * 6x^2 + 2 * 3x - 2 * 2 =$
$2(6x^2 + 3x - 2)$

We look at every polynomial member as a product of a real number and a variable. Notice that all real numbers in the

polynomial are even, so they have the same number (factor).
We pull out that 2 in front of the polynomial, and we write
what is left.

What if have a more complex case, where we can't find a factor that is a real number? Here is an example:

$$x^2 - 2x + 1 =$$
$$x^2 - x - x + 1 =$$
$$x(x - 1) - (x - 1) =$$
$$(x - 1)(x - 1)$$

We can write -2x as –x-x . Now we group first 2 members
and we see that they have the same factor x, which we can
pull in front of them. For the other 2 members, we pull the
minus in front of them, so we can get the same binomial
that we got with the first 2 members. Now we have that this
binomial is the factor for x(x-1) and (x-1).

If we pull x-1 in front (underlined), from the first member we
are left with x, and from the second we have -1.
And that is how we transform a polynomial into a product of
2 polynomials (in this case binomials).

Quadratic equations

A. Factoring

Quadratic equations are usually called second degree equations, which mean that the second degree is the highest
degree of the variable that can be found in the quadratic
equation. The form of these equations is:

$$ax^2 + bx + c = 0$$

where a, b and c are some real numbers.

One way for solving quadratic equations is the factoring
method, where we transform the quadratic equation into a
product of 2 or more polynomials. Let's see how that works
in one simple example:

$x^2 + 2x = 0$
$x(x + 2) = 0$
$(x = 0)$ V $(x + 2 = 0)$
$(x = 0$ V $(x + -2)$

Notice that here we don't have parameter c, but this is still a quadratic equation, because we have the second degree of variable x. Our factor here is x, which we put in front and we are left with x+2. The equation is equal to 0, so either x or x+2 are 0, or both are 0.
So, our 2 solutions are 0 and -2.

B. Quadratic formula

If we are unsure how to rewrite quadratic equations so we can solve it using factoring method, we can use the formula for quadratic equation:

$$x_{1,2} = \frac{-b \pm \sqrt{b^2 - 4ac}}{2a}$$

We write $x_{1,2}$ because it represents 2 solutions of the equation. Here is one example:

$3x^2 - 10x + 3 = 0$

$x_{1,2} = \frac{-b \pm \sqrt{b^2 - 4ac}}{2a}$

We see that a is 3, b is -10 and c is 3.

$x_{1,2} = \frac{-(-10) \pm \sqrt{(-10)^2 - 4 \cdot 3 \cdot 3}}{2 \cdot 3}$

We use these numbers in the equation and do some calculations.

$x_{1,2} = \frac{10 \pm \sqrt{100 - 36}}{6}$

$x_{1,2} = \frac{10 \pm \sqrt{64}}{6}$

$x_{1,2} = \frac{10 \pm 8}{6}$

Notice that we have + and -, so x_1 is for + and x_2 is for -, and that's how we get 2 solutions.

$x_1 = \frac{10 + 8}{6} = \frac{18}{6} = 3$

$x_2 = \frac{10 - 8}{6} = \frac{2}{6} = \frac{1}{3}$

Cartesian Plane, Coordinate Plane and Coordinate Grid

To locate dots and draw lines and curves, we use the coordinate plane. It also called Cartesian coordinate plane. It is a two-dimensional surface with a coordinate grid in it, which helps us to count the units. For the counting of those units, we use x-axis (horizontal scale) and y-axis (vertical scale).

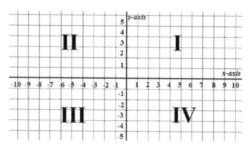

The whole system is called a coordinate system which is divided into 4 parts, called quadrants. The quadrant where all numbers are positive is the 1st quadrant (I), and if we go counterclockwise, we mark all 4 quadrants.

The location of a dot in the coordinate system is represented by coordinates. Coordinates are represented as a pair of numbers, where the 1st number is located on the x-axis and the 2nd number is located on the y-axis. So, if a dot A has coordinates a and b, then we write:

A=(a,b)   or   A(a,b)

The point where x-axis and y-axis intersect is called an origin. The origin is the point from which we measure the distance along the x and y axes.

In the Cartesian coordinate system we can calculate the distance between 2 given points. If we have dots with coordinates:

$\begin{cases} A=(a,b) \\ B=(c,d) \end{cases}$

Then the distance d between A and B can be calculated by the following formula:

$$d = \sqrt{(c-a)^2 + (d-b)^2}$$

Cartesian coordinate system is used for the drawing of 2-dimentional shapes, and is also commonly used for functions.

Example:

Draw the function   y = (1 - x)/2

To draw a linear function, we need at least 2 points.
If we put that x=0 then value for y would be:

$$y = \frac{1-x}{2} = \frac{1-0}{2} = \frac{1}{2}$$

We found the 1st point, let's name it A, with following coordinates:

A = (0,1/2)

To find the 2nd point, we can put that x=1. Here, the value for y would be:

$$y = \frac{1-x}{2} = \frac{1-1}{2} = \frac{0}{2} = 0$$

If we denote the 2nd point with B, then the coordinates for this point are:

B=(1,0)

Since we have 2 points necessary for the function, we find them in the coordinate system and we connect them with a line that represents the function,

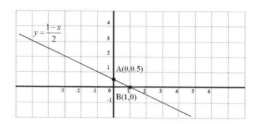

Perimeter Area and Volume

Perimeter and Area (2-dimentional shapes)

Perimeter of a shape determines the length around that shape, while the area includes the space inside the shape.

Rectangle:

P = 2a + 2b
A = ab

Square

P = 4a
A = a^2

Parallelogram

P = 2a + 2b
A = ah_a = bh_b

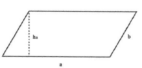

Rhombus

P = 4a
A = ah = $d_1d_2/2$

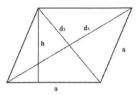

Triangle

P = a + b + c
A = $ah_a/2$ = $bh_b/2$ = $ch_c/2$

Equilateral Triangle

P = 3a
A = $(a^2\sqrt{3})/4$

Trapezoid

P = a + b + c + d
A = ((a + b)/2)h

Circle

P = 2r $\prod$
A = $r^2 \prod$

Area and Volume (3-dimentional shapes)

To calculate the area of a 3-dimentional shape, we calculate the areas of all sides and then we add them all.

To find the volume of a 3-dimentional shape, we multiply the area of the base (B) and the height (H) of the 3-dimentional shape.

$$V = BH$$

In case of a pyramid and a cone, the volume would be divided by 3.

$$V = BH/3$$

Here are some of the 3-dimentional shapes with formulas for their area and volume:

Cuboids

$A = 2(ab + bc + ac)$
$V = abc$

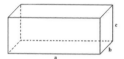

Cube

$A = 6a^2$
$V = a^3$

Pyramid

$A = ab + ah_a + bh_b$

$V = abH/3$

Cylinder

$A = 2r^2 \prod + 2r\prod H$
$V = r^2\prod H$

Cone

$A = (r + s)r\prod$
$V = (r^2\prod H)/3$

Pythagorean Geometry

If we have a right triangle ABC, where its sides (legs) are a and b and c is a hypotenuse (the side opposite the right angle), then we can establish a relationship between these sides using the following formula:

$c^2 = a^2 + b^2$

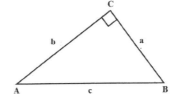

This formula is proven in the Pythagorean Theorem. There are many proofs of this theorem, but we'll look at just one geometrical proof:

If we draw squares on the right triangle's sides, then the area of the square upon the hypotenuse is equal to the sum of the areas of the squares that are upon other two sides of the triangle. Since the areas of these squares are a^2, b^2 and c^2, that is how we got the formula above.

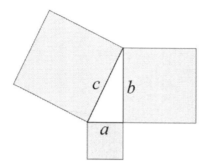

One of the famous right triangles is one with sides 3, 4 and 5. And we can see here that:

$3^2 + 4^2 = 5^2$
$9 + 16 = 25$
$25 = 25$

Example Problem:

The isosceles triangle ABC has a perimeter of 18 centimeters, and the difference between its base and legs is 3 centimeters. Find the height of this triangle.

We write the information we have about triangle ABC and we draw a picture of it for better understanding of the relation

between its elements:

P=18 cm
a - b = 3 cm
h=?

We use the formula for the perimeter of the isosceles triangle, since that is what is given to us:

P=a+2b=18 cm

Notice that we have 2 equations with 2 variables, so we can solve it as a system of equations:

a + 2b = 18
a − b = 3 / a + 2b = 18
2a - 2b = 6 / a + 2b + 2a - 2b = 18 + 6
3a = 24
a = 24/3 = 8 cm

Now we go back to find b:
a - b = 3
8 - b = 3
b = 8 - 3
b = 5 cm

Using Pythagorean Theorem, we can find the height using a and b, because the height falls on the side a at the right angle. Notice that height cuts side a exactly in half, and that's why we use in the formula a/2. In this case, b is our hypotenuse, so we have:

$b^2 = (a/2)^2 + h^2$
$h^2 = b^2 - (a/2)^2$
$h^2 = 5^2 - (8/2)^2$
$h^2 = 5^2 - (8/2)^2$
$h^2 = 25 - 4^2$
$h^2 = 26 - 16$
$h^2 = 9$
h = 3 cm.

Quadrilaterals

Quadrilaterals are 2-dimentional geometrical shapes that have 4 sides and 4 angles. There are many types of quadrilaterals, depending on the length of its sides and if they are parallel and also depending on the size of its angles. All quadrilaterals have the following properties:

Sum of all interior angles is 360^0

Sum of all exterior angles is 360^0

A quadrilateral is a parallelogram is it fulfills at least one of the following conditions:

Angles on each side are supplementary
Opposite angles are equal
Opposite sides are equal
Diagonals intersect each other exactly in half

Here are some of the quadrilaterals:

Square

All sides are equal
All angles are right angles

Rectangle

2 pairs of equal sides
All angles are right angles

Parallelogram

2 pairs of equal sides
Opposite angles are equal

Rhombus

All sides are equal
Opposite angles are equal

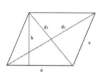

Trapezoid

One pair of parallel sides

Example Problem

Find all angles of a parallelogram if one angle is greater than the other one by 40^0.

First, we draw an image of a parallelogram:

We denote angles by α and β, Since this is a parallelogram, the opposite angles are equal.

We are given that one angle is greater than the other one by 40^0, so we can write:

$\beta = \alpha + 40^0$

We solve this problem in two ways:
1) The sum of all internal angles of every quadrilateral is 360^0. There are 2 α and 2 β. So we have:
$2\alpha + 2\beta = 360^0$

Now, instead of β we write $\alpha + 40$:
$2\alpha + 2\ (\alpha + 40^0) = 360^0$
$2\alpha + 2\alpha + 80^0 = 360^0$
$4\alpha = 360^0 - 80^0$
$4\alpha = 280^0$
$\alpha = 280^0\ /\ 4$
$\alpha = 70^0$
Now we can find β from α:
$\beta = \alpha + 40^0$
$\beta = 70^0 + 40^0$
$\beta = 110^0$

2) One of the conditions for parallelogram is " Angles on each side are supplementary" and we can use that to find these angles:
$\alpha + \beta = 180^0$
$\alpha + \alpha + 40^0 = 180^0$

$2\alpha = 180^0 - 40^0$
$2\alpha = 140^0$
$\alpha = 70^0$

Now we find β:
$\beta = \alpha + 40^0$
$\beta = 70^0 + 40^0$
$\beta = 110^0$

Writing

THIS SECTION CONTAINS A SELF-ASSESSMENT AND WRIT-ING SKILLS TUTORIALS. The tutorials are designed to familiarize general principles and the self-assessment contains general questions similar to the writing skills questions likely to be on the PERT exam, but are not intended to be identical to the exam questions. The tutorials are not designed to be a complete course, and it is assumed that students have some familiarity with writing skills. If you do not understand parts of the tutorial, or find the tutorial difficult, it is recommended that you seek out additional instruction.

Tour of the PERT Writing Content

The PERT writing skills section has 20 questions. Below is a list of the likely writing skills topics likely to appear on the PERT. Make sure that you understand these topics at the very minimum.

- English grammar

- English usage

- Punctuation

- Subject - verb agreement

- Sentence structure

The questions in the self-assessment are not the same as you will find on the PERT - that would be too easy! And nobody knows what the questions will be and they change all the time. Mostly, the changes consist of substituting new questions for old, but the changes also can be new question formats or styles, changes to the number of questions in each section, changes to the time limits for each section, and combining sections. So, while the format and exact wording of the questions may differ slightly, and changes from year to year, if you can answer the questions below, you will have no problem with the writing skills section of the PERT.

Writing Self-Assessment

The purpose of the self-assessment is:

- Identify your strengths and weaknesses.

- Develop your personalized study plan (above)

- Get accustomed to the PERT format

- Extra practice – the self-assessments are almost a full 3rd practice test!

- Provide a baseline score for preparing your study schedule.

Since this is a Self-assessment, and depending on how confident you are with writing skills, timing yourself is optional. The PERT has 20 questions. This self-assessment has 25 questions, so allow about 20 minutes to complete.

Once complete, use the table below to assess your understanding of the content, and prepare your study schedule described in chapter 1.

80% - 100%	Excellent – you have mastered the content
60 – 79%	Good. You have a working knowledge. Even though you can just pass this section, you may want to review the tutorials and do some extra practice to see if you can improve your mark.
40% - 59%	Below Average. You do not understand the content. Review the tutorials , and retake this quiz again in a few days, before proceeding to the practice test questions.
Less than 40%	Poor. You have a very limited understanding. Please review the tutorials , and retake this quiz again in a few days, before proceeding to the practice test questions.

Writing Answer Sheet

1. Ⓐ Ⓑ Ⓒ Ⓓ   11. Ⓐ Ⓑ Ⓒ Ⓓ   21. Ⓐ Ⓑ Ⓒ Ⓓ

2. Ⓐ Ⓑ Ⓒ Ⓓ   12. Ⓐ Ⓑ Ⓒ Ⓓ   22. Ⓐ Ⓑ Ⓒ Ⓓ

3. Ⓐ Ⓑ Ⓒ Ⓓ   13. Ⓐ Ⓑ Ⓒ Ⓓ   23. Ⓐ Ⓑ Ⓒ Ⓓ

4. Ⓐ Ⓑ Ⓒ Ⓓ   14. Ⓐ Ⓑ Ⓒ Ⓓ   24. Ⓐ Ⓑ Ⓒ Ⓓ

5. Ⓐ Ⓑ Ⓒ Ⓓ   15. Ⓐ Ⓑ Ⓒ Ⓓ   25. Ⓐ Ⓑ Ⓒ Ⓓ

6. Ⓐ Ⓑ Ⓒ Ⓓ   16. Ⓐ Ⓑ Ⓒ Ⓓ

7. Ⓐ Ⓑ Ⓒ Ⓓ   17. Ⓐ Ⓑ Ⓒ Ⓓ

8. Ⓐ Ⓑ Ⓒ Ⓓ   18. Ⓐ Ⓑ Ⓒ Ⓓ

9. Ⓐ Ⓑ Ⓒ Ⓓ   19. Ⓐ Ⓑ Ⓒ Ⓓ

10. Ⓐ Ⓑ Ⓒ Ⓓ   20. Ⓐ Ⓑ Ⓒ Ⓓ

1. Choose the sentence that is written correctly.

a. The older children have already eat their dinner, but the baby has not yet eaten anything.

b. The older children have already eaten their dinner, but the baby has not yet ate anything.

c. The older children have already eaten their dinner, but the baby has not eaten anything yet.

d. None of the sentences are correct.

2. Choose the sentence that is written correctly.

a. Its important for you to know its official name; its called the Confederate Museum.

b. It's important for you to know it's official name; it's called the Confederate Museum.

c. It's important for you to know its official name; it's called the Confederate Museum.

d. None of the sentences are correct.

3. Choose the sentence that is written correctly.

a. None of the sentences are correct.

b. If he would have known about the forecast, he would have postponed the camping trip.

c. If he have known about the forecast, he would have postponed the camping trip.

d. If he had known about the forecast, he would have postponed the camping trip.

4. Choose the sentence that is written correctly.

a. He doesn't have any money to buy clothes and neither do I.

b. He doesn't have any money to buy clothes and neither does I.

c. He don't have any money to buy clothes and neither does I.

d. None of the sentences are correct.

5. Choose the sentence that is written correctly.

a. Because it really don't matter, I don't care if I go there.

b. Because it really doesn't matter, I don't care if I go there.

c. Because it really don't matter, I don't care if I go there.

d. No change is necessary

6. Choose the sentence that is written correctly.

a. The mother would not of punished her daughter if she could have avoided it.

b. The mother would not have punished her daughter if she could of avoided it.

c. No changes are necessary.

d. The mother would not have punished her daughter if she could have avoided it.

7. Choose the sentence that is written correctly.

a. There was scarcely no food in the pantry, because nobody ate at home.

b. There was scarcely any food in the pantry, because nobody ate at home.

c. There was scarcely any food in the pantry, because not nobody ate at home.

d. No changes are necessary.

8. Choose the sentence that is written correctly.

a. Michael has lived in that house for forty years, while I has owned this one for only six weeks.

b. Michael have lived in that house for forty years, while I have owned this one for only six weeks.

c. Michael have lived in that house for forty years, while I has owned this one for only six weeks.

d. None of the sentences are correct.

9. Choose the word that best completes the sentence below.

Lee pronounced _____ name incorrectly; it's an impatiens, not an impatience.

a. it's

b. its

c. A or B

d. None of the above.

10. Choose the word that best completes the sentence below.

After the car was fixed it _____ again.

   a. None of the choices are correct.

   b. ran well

   c. would have run well

   d. ran more well

11. Choose the sentence that is written correctly..

   a. Ted and Janice, who had been friends for years, went on vacation together every summer.

   b. Ted and Janice who had been friends for years, went on vacation together every summer.

   c. Ted, and Janice who had been friends for years, went on vacation together every summer.

   d. None of the choices are correct.

12. Choose the sentence that is written correctly.

   a. None of us want to go to the party not even, if there will be live music.

   b. None of us want to go to the party, not even if there will be live music.

   c. None of us want to go to the party; not even if there will be live music.

   d. None of the choice are correct.

13. Choose the sentence that is written correctly.

   a. John, Maurice, and Thomas quit school two months before graduation.

   b. John, Maurice and Thomas quit school two months before graduation.

   c. John Maurice and Thomas, quit school two months before graduation.

   d. None of the choice are correct.

14. Choose the sentence that is written correctly.

a. "My father said that he would be there on Sunday" Lee explained.

b. None of the choices are correct.

c. "My father said that he would be there on Sunday," Lee explained.

d. "My father said that he would be there on Sunday." Lee explained.

15. Choose the sentence that is written correctly.

a. I own two dogs, a cat named Jeffrey, and Henry, the goldfish.

b. I own two dogs a cat, named Jeffrey, and Henry, the goldfish.

c. I own two dogs, a cat named Jeffrey; and Henry, the goldfish.

d. None of the choices are correct.

16. Choose the sentence below with the correct punctuation.

a.   Marcus who won the debate tournament, is the best speaker that I know.

b.   Marcus, who won the debate tournament, is the best speaker that I know.

c.   Marcus who won the debate tournament is the best speaker that I know.

d.   Marcus who won the debate tournament is the best speaker, that I know.

17. The ceremony had an emotional _____ on the groom, but the bride was not <u>affected</u>.

    a. effect

    b. affect

    c. None of the choices are correct.

18. Choose the sentence that is written correctly.

    a. None of the choices are correct.

    b. Anna was taller then Luis, but than he grew four inches in three months.

    c. Anna was taller than Luis, but than he grew four inches, in three months.

    d. Anna was taller than Luis, but then he grew four inches in three months.

19. Choose the word that best completes the sentence below.

There second home is in Boca Raton, but _____ not there for most of the year.

    a. Their

    b. There

    c. They're

    d. None of the choices are correct.

20. Choose the word that best completes the sentence below.

Their going to graduate in June; after that, their best option will be to go _____.

    a. There

    b. They're

    c. Their

    d. None of the choices are correct.

21. Choose the word that best completes the sentence below.

Your mistaken; that is not _____ book.

    a. You are

    b. Your

    c. You're

    d. None of the choices are correct.

22. Choose the word that best completes the sentence below.

You're classes are on the west side of campus, but _____ living on the east side.

    a. Your

    b. You're

    c. None of the choices are correct.

23. Choose the sentence that is written correctly.

    a. The Chinese live in one of the world's most populous nations, while a citizen of Bermuda lives in one of the least populous.

    b. The Chinese lives in one of the world's most populous nations, while a citizen of Bermuda live in one of the least populous.

    c. The Chinese live in one of the world's most populous nations, while a citizen of Bermuda live in one of the least populous.

    d. None of the choices are correct.

24. Choose the sentence that is written correctly.

a. You shouldn't sit in that chair wearing black pants; I set the white cat there just a moment ago.

b. You shouldn't set in that chair wearing black pants; I sit the white cat there just a moment ago.

c. You shouldn't set in that chair wearing black pants; I set the white cat there just a moment ago.

d. None of the choices are correct.

25. Choose the sentence that is written correctly.

a. Golden Gate Bridge in San Francisco

b. golden gate bridge in San Francisco

c. Golden gate bridge in San Francisco

d. None of the choice are correct.

Answer Key

1. C
Present perfect. You cannot use the Present Perfect with specific time expressions such as: yesterday, one year ago, last week, when I was a child, at that moment, that day, one day, etc. The Present Perfect is used with unspecific expressions such as: ever, never, once, many times, several times, before, so far, already, yet, etc.

2. C
Its vs. It's. "It's" is a contraction for it is or it has. "Its" is a possessive pronoun meaning, more or less, of it or belonging to it.

3. D
The third conditional is used for talking about an unreal situation (that did not happen) in the past. For example, "If I had studied harder, [if clause] I would have passed the exam [main clause]. Which is the same as, "I failed the exam, because I didn't study hard enough."

4. A
Disagreeing with a negative statement uses "neither."

5. B
Doesn't, does not, or does is used with the third person singular--words like he, she, and it. Don't, do not, or do is used for other subjects.

6. D
The third conditional is used for talking about an unreal situation (that did not happen) in the past. For example, "If I had studied harder, [if clause] I would have passed the exam [main clause]. Which is the same as, "I failed the exam, because I didn't study hard enough."

7. B
Double negative sentence. In double negative sentences, one of the negatives is replaced with "any."

8. D
Present perfect. You cannot use the Present Perfect with specific time expressions such as: yesterday, one year ago, last week, when I was a child, at that moment, that day, one day, etc. The Present Perfect is used with unspecific expressions such as: ever, never, once, many times, several times, before, so far, already, yet, etc.

9. B
Its vs. It's. "It's" is a contraction for it is or it has. "Its" is a possessive pronoun meaning, more or less, of it or belonging to it.

10. B
Present tense, "ran well" is correct. "Ran good" is never correct.

11. A
Use a comma to separate phrases.

12. B
Use a comma separates independent clauses. None of us wants to go to the party, not even if there will be live music.

13. B
Don't use a comma before 'and' in a list.

14. C
Commas always go with a quote and the use of said, explained etc.

15. A
This is an example if a comma which appears before 'and,' but is disambiguating. Without the comma, the sentence would be "I own two dogs, a cat named Jeffrey and Henry, the goldfish." This means there is a cat named Jeffrey and Henry, and a goldfish with no name mentioned. The comma appears to show the distinction.

I own two dogs, a cat named Jeffrey, and Henry, the goldfish.

16. B
Comma separate phrases.

17. A
Affect vs. Effect - "Affect" is a verb (action) and "effect" is a noun (thing).

18. D
Than vs. Then – Than is used for comparison, as in, taller than, and then is used for time, as in, but then...

19. C
There vs. their vs. they're. "There" indicates existence as in, "there are." "Their" indicates possession, as in, "their book." "They're" is the contraction form of "they are."

20. A
There vs. their vs. they're. "There" indicates existence as in, "there are." "Their" indicates possession, as in, "their book." "They're" is the contraction form of "they are."

21. B
Your vs. you're. "Your" is the possessive form of you. "You're" is the contraction form of you are.

22. B
Your vs. you're. "Your" is the possessive form of you. "You're" is the contraction form of you are.

23. A
Singular subjects. "The Chinese" is plural, and "a citizen of Bermuda" is singular.

24. A
Sit vs. Set. Set requires an object – something to set down. "Sit" is something that you do, like sit on the chair.

25. A
Always capitalize proper nouns.

Common English Usage Mistakes - A Quick Review

Like some parts of English grammar, usage is definitely going to be on the exam and there isn't any tricky strategies or shortcuts to help you get through this section.
Here is a quick review of common usage mistakes.

1. May and Might

'May' can act as a principal verb, which can express permission or possibility.

Examples:

Lets wait, the meeting may have started.
May I begin now?

'May' can act as an auxiliary verb, which an expresses a purpose or wish

Examples:

May you find favour in the sight of your employer.

May your wishes come true.
People go to school so that they may be educated.

The past tense of may is might.

Examples:

I asked if I might begin

'Might' can be used to signify a weak or slim possibility or polite suggestion.

Examples:

You might find him in his office, but I doubt it.
You might offer to help if you want to.

2. Lie and Lay

The verb lay should always take an object. The three forms of the verb lay are: laid, lay and laid.

The verb lie (recline) should not take any object. The three forms of the verb lie are: lay, lie and lain.

Examples:

Lay on the bed.
The tables were laid by the students.
Let the little kid lie.
The patient lay on the table.

The dog has lain there for 30 minutes.

Note: The verb lie can also mean "to tell a falsehood". This verb can appear in three forms: lied, lie, and lied. This is different from the verb lie (recline) mentioned above.

Examples:

The accused is fond of telling lies.
Did she lie?

3. Would and should

The past tense of shall is 'should', and so "should" generally follows the same principles as "shall."

The past tense of will is "would," and so "would" generally follows the same principles as "will."

The two verbs 'would and should' can be correctly used

interchangeably to signify obligation. The two verbs also have some unique uses too. Should is used in three persons to signify obligation.

Examples:

I should go after work.
People should do exercises everyday.
You should be generous.

"Would" is specially used in any of the three persons, to signify willingness, determination and habitual action.
Examples:

They would go for a test run every Saturday.
They would not ignore their duties.
She would try to be punctual.

4. Principle and Auxiliary Verbs

Two principal verbs can be used along with one auxiliary verb as long as the auxiliary verb form suits the two principal verbs.

Examples:

A number of people have been employed and some promoted.

A new tree has been planted and the old has been cut down. Again note the difference in the verb form.

5. Can and Could

A. Can is used to express capacity or ability.

Examples:

I can complete the assignment today

He can meet up with his target.

B. Can is also used to express permission.

Examples:

Yes, you can begin

In the sentence below, "can" was used to mean the same thing as "may." However, the difference is that the word "can" is used for negative or interrogative sentences, while "may" is used in affirmative sentences to express possibility.

Examples:

They may be correct.   Positive sentence - use may.
Can this statement be correct? A question using "can."
It cannot be correct. Negative sentence using "can."

The past tense of can is could. It can serve as a principal verb when it is used to express its own meaning.

Examples:

In spite of the difficulty of the test, he could still perform well.
"Could" here is used to express ability.

6. Ought

The verb ought should normally be followed by the word to.

Examples:

I *ought to* close shop now.

The verb 'ought' can be used to express:

A. Desirability
You ought to wash your hands before eating.   It is desirable to wash your hands.

B. Probability
She ought to be on her way back by now. She is probably on her way.

C. Moral obligation or duty
The government ought to protect the oppressed. It is the government's duty to protect the oppressed.

7. Raise and Rise

Rise
The verb rise means to go up, or to ascend.
The verb rise can appear in three forms, rose, rise, and risen. The verb should not take an object.

Examples:

The bird rose very slowly.
The trees rise above the house.
My aunt has risen in her career.

Raise
The verb raise means to increase, to lift up.
The verb raise can appear in three forms, raised, raise and raised.

Examples:

He raised his hand.
The workers requested a raise.
Do not raise that subject.

8. Past Tense and Past Participle

Pay attention to the proper use these verbs: sing, show, ring, awake, fly, flow, begin, hang and sink.

Mistakes usually occur when using the past participle and past tense of these verbs as they are often mixed up.

Each of these verbs can appear in three forms:

Sing, Sang, Sung.
Show, Showed, Showed/Shown.
Ring, Rang, Rung.
Awake, awoke, awaken
Fly, Flew, Flown.
Flow, Flowed, Flowed.
Begin, Began, Begun.
Hang, Hanged, Hanged (a criminal)
Hang, Hung, Hung (a picture)
Sink, Sank, Sunk.

Examples:

The stranger rang the door bell. (simple past tense)
I have rung the door bell already. (past participle - an action completed in the past)

The stone sank in the river. (simple past tense)
The stone had already sunk. (past participle - an action completed in the past)

The meeting began at 4:00.
The meeting has begun.

9. Shall and Will

When speaking informally, the two can be used interchangeably. In formal writing, they must be used correctly.

"Will" is used in the second or third person, while "shall" is used in the first person. Both verbs are used to express a time or even in the future.

Examples:

I shall, We shall (First Person)
You will (Second Person)
They will (Third Person)

This principle however reverses when the verbs are to be used to express threats, determination, command, willingness, promise or compulsion. In these instances, will is now used in first person and shall in the second and third person.

Examples:

I will be there next week, no matter what.
This is a promise, so the first person "I" takes "will."

You shall ensure that the work is completed.
This is a command, so the second person "you" takes "shall."

I will try to make payments as promised.
This is a promise, so the first person "I" takes "will."

They shall have arrived by the end of the day.
This is a determination, so the third person "they" takes shall.

Note
A. The two verbs, shall and will should not occur twice in the same sentence when the same future is being referred to

Example:

I shall arrive early if my driver is here on time.

B. Will should not be used in the first person when questions are being asked

Examples:

Shall I go ?
Shall we go?

Subject Verb Agreement

Verbs in any sentence must agree with the subject of the sentence both in person and number. Problems usually occur when the verb doesn't correspond to the right subject or the verb fails to match the noun close to it.

Unfortunately, there is no easy way around these principals - no tricky strategy or easy rule.   You just have to memorize them.

Here is a quick review:

The verb to be, present (past)

Person	Singular	Plural
First	I am (was)	we are (were)
Second	you are (were)	you are (were)
Third	he, she, it is (was)	they are (were)

The verb to have, present (past)

Person	Singular	Plural
First	I have (had)	we have (had)
Second	you have (had)	you have (had)
Third	he, she, it has (had)	they have (had)

Regular verbs, e.g. to walk, present (past)

Person	Singular	Plural
First	I walk (walked)	we walk (walked)

| Second | you walk (walked) | you walk (walked) |
| Third | he, she, it walks (walked) | they work (walked) |

1. Every and Each

When nouns are qualified by "every" or "each," they take a singular verb even if they are joined by 'and'

Examples:

Each mother and daughter *was* a given separate test.
Every teacher and student *was* properly welcomed.

2. Plural Nouns

Nouns like measles, tongs, trousers, riches, scissors etc. are all plural.

Examples:

The trousers *are* dirty.
My scissors *have* gone missing.
The tongs *are* on the table.

3. With and As Well

Two subjects linked by "with" or "as well" should have a verb that matches the first subject.

Examples:

The pencil, with the papers and equipment, *is* on the desk.
David as well as Louis is coming.

4. Plural Nouns

The following nouns take a singular verb:

> politics, mathematics, innings, news, advice,
> summons, furniture, information, poetry, machinery,
> vacation, scenery

Examples:

The machinery *is* difficult to assemble
The furniture *has* been delivered
The scenery *was* beautiful

5. Single Entities

A proper noun in plural form that refers to a single entity requires a singular verb. This is a complicated way of saying;
some things appear to be plural, but are really singular, or
some nouns refer to a collection of things but the collection
is really singular.

Examples:

The United Nations Organization *is* the decision maker in
the matter.

Here the "United Nations Organization" is really only one
"thing" or noun, but is made up of many "nations."

The book, "The Seven Virgins" *was* not available in the
library.

Here there is only one book, although the title of the book is
plural.

6. Specific Amounts are always singular

A plural noun that refers to a specific amount or quantity that is considered as a whole (dozen, hundred, score etc) requires a singular verb.

Examples:

60 minutes *is* quite a long time.
Here "60 minutes" is considered a whole, and therefore one item (singular noun).

The first million is the most difficult.

7. Either, Neither and Each are always singular

The verb is always singular when used with: either, each, neither, every one and many.

Examples:

Either of the boys *is* lying.
Each of the employees *has* been well compensated
Many a police officer *has* been found to be courageous
Every one of the teachers *is* responsible

8. Linking with Either, Or, and Neither match the second subject

Two subjects linked by "either," "or,""nor" or "neither" should have a verb that matches the second subject.

Examples:

Neither David nor Paul *will* be coming.
Either Mary or Tina *is* paying.

Note

If one of the subjects linked by "either," "or,""nor" or "neither" is in plural form, then the verb should also be in plural, and the verb should be close to the plural subject.

Examples:

Neither the mother *nor* her kids *have* eaten.
Either Mary *or* her *friends are* paying.

9. Collective Nouns are Plural

Some collective nouns such as poultry, gentry, cattle, vermin etc. are considered plural and require a plural verb.

Examples:

The *poultry are* sick.
The *cattle are* well fed.

Note

Collective nouns involving people can work with both plural and singular verbs.

Examples:

Nigerians are known to be hard working
Europeans live in Africa

10. Nouns that are Singular and Plural

Nouns like deer, sheep, swine, salmon etc. can be singular or plural and require the same verb form.

Examples:

The swine is feeding. (singular)
The swine are feeding. (plural)

The salmon is on the table. (singular)
The salmon are running upstream. (plural)

11. Collective Nouns are Singular

Collective nouns such as Army, Jury, Assembly, Committee, Team etc should carry a singular verb when they subscribe to one idea. If the ideas or views are more than one, then the verb used should be plural.

Examples:

The committee is in agreement in their decision.

The committee were in disagreement in their decision.
The jury has agreed on a verdict.
The jury were unable to agree on a verdict.

12. Subjects links by "and" are plural.

Two subjects linked by "and" always require a plural verb

Examples:

David and John are students.

Note
If the subjects linked by "and" are used as one phrase, or constitute one idea, then the verb must be singular

The color of his socks and shoe is black.
Here "socks and shoe" are two nouns, however the subject is "color" which is singular.

Punctuation - Colons, Semicolons, Hyphens, Dashes, Parentheses and Apostrophes

Within a sentence there are several different types of punctuation marks that can denote a pause. Each of these punctuation marks has different rules when it comes to its structure and usage, so we will look at each one in turn.

Colons

The colon is used primarily to introduce information. It can start lists such as in the sentence, "There were several things Susan had to get at the store: bread, cereal, lettuce and tomatoes." Or a colon points out specific information, such as in the sentence, "It was only then that the group fully realized what had happened: The Martian invasion had begun."

Note that if the information after the colon is a complete sentence, you capitalize and punctuate it exactly like you would a sentence. If, however, it does not constitute a complete sentence, you don't have to capitalize anything. ("Peering out the window Meredith saw them: zombies.")

Semicolons

Semicolons can be thought of as super commas. They denote a stronger stop than a comma does, but they are still weaker than a period, not quite capable of ending a sentence. Semicolons are primarily used to separate independent clauses that are not being separated by a coordinating conjunction. ("Chris went to the store; he bought chips and salsa.") Semicolons can only do this, however, when the ideas in each clause are related. For instance, the sentence, "It's raining outside; my sister went to the movies," is not a proper usage of the semicolon since those clauses have nothing to do with each other.

Semicolons can also be used in lists provided that one or more element in the list is itself made up of a smaller list.

If you want to write a list of things you plan to bring to a picnic, and those things only include a Frisbee, a chair and some pasta salad, you would not need to use a semicolon. But if you also wanted to bring plastic knives, forks and spoons, you would need to write your sentence like this: "For our picnic I am bringing a Frisbee; a chair; plastic knives, forks and spoons; and some pasta salad."

Using semicolons like this preserves the smaller list that you have in your larger list.

Hyphens

To join words together to show that they are linked you use hyphens. The most common use of hyphens is to link together words to show that they are working together in a sentence. ("The well-known actor was eating at the table behind us.") This shows explicitly that you are using "well-known" as a single concept and not as two descriptive words in a list.

Hyphens can also be used to split a word in half if you run out of space writing on one line of a page. This is often seen in newspapers and magazines when text is justified to both sides of a page or a column. For example:

The massive earthquake caused surpris-

ingly little damage in the affected areas.

However, you can only use a hyphen in this way if you split the word between syllables. Often students think that they can use hyphens to break up words wherever they want; this is wrong. For the word "surprisingly" you

could have a hyphen between "sur" and "prisingly," "surpris" and "ingly, and between "surprising" and "ly," but nowhere else.

Finally, hyphens can be used to add prefixes to words. This

happens a lot in news reports with phrases such as "pro-government troops."

Dashes and Parentheses

Both dashes and parentheses are used to set aside information into parenthetical statements; statements that can be treated as an aside. They do not need to be there for the sentence to make sense, but the information they provide is interesting enough that you feel it should be included. Parentheses are considered stronger than dashes are. (Commas can also be used to separate nonessential information from a sentence, but they are considered to be the weakest of the three.)

As the previous sentence shows, parentheses can surround entire sentences, separating them from the paragraph. Dashes, on the other hand, can separate off the last statement in a sentence. ("Calvin came home and greeted his family for the first time in days—everyone smiled.") Obviously, that last sentence could also be written using a semicolon or as two sentences. The difference is in how you want it to sound to the reader. Should these thoughts be treated as two distinct pieces? Or should everyone smiling at Calvin be part of the main sentence, just separated a bit more strongly—with a slightly longer pause—than a comma could manage?

Apostrophes

There are two primary uses of the apostrophe in English: forming contractions and forming possessive nouns.

Contractions are formed by taking two words and combining them together with an apostrophe replacing the missing letters (do not becomes don't), or by shortening an existing word (cannot becomes can't). Apostrophes can

also make contractions by attaching verbs to nouns or pronouns. ("He's going to the store.")

When making singular nouns possessive the general rule is that you add an 's to the end of singular nouns. (This is Tim's bagel.) When dealing with plural nouns that do not end with the letter –s (such as children), the rule is that you also add an 's to the end of the word. (It was the children's favorite movie.) And when dealing with plural nouns that end with the letter –s, you simply add an apostrophe. (My sisters' favorite game is tag.)

However, and this is an important "however" given the controversy it can cause, when dealing with singular words that end with the letter –s (such as circus), there are two standards for how to make them possessive—each with its own grammar books to back it up.

One standard says that you still add an 's to the end of the word. (This is the circus's biggest tent.) The other says that, since the word ends with an –s, it can only get an apostrophe. (This is the circus' biggest tent.) Some style books, such as the Chicago Manual of Style will go so far as to say that the former option is correct, but to avoid inflaming people's passions on the subject, using the latter is perfectly acceptable. The best thing to do is to find out which style the teacher or editor you are writing for at any given time prefers and conform to it for that person.

Commas

Commas are probably the most commonly used punctuation mark in English. Commas can break the flow of writing to give it a more natural sounding style, and they are the main punctuation mark used to separate ideas. Commas also separate lists, introductory adverbs, introductory prepositional phrases, dates and addresses.

The most rigid way that commas are used is when separating clauses. There are two primary types of clauses in a sentence, independent and subordinate (sometimes called dependent). Independent clauses are clauses that express a complete thought such as, "Tim went to the store." Subordinate clauses, on the other hand, only express partial thoughts that serve to expand upon an independent clause such as, "after the game ended," which you can see is clearly not a complete sentence. (You will learn more about clauses in different lessons.)

The rule for commas with clauses is that a comma must separate the clauses when a subordinate clause comes first in a sentence: "After the game ended, Tim went to the store." But there should not be a comma when a subordinate clause follows an independent clause: "Tim went to the store after the game ended." If you leave the comma out of the first example, you have a run-on sentence. If you add one into the second example, you have a comma-splice error. Also, when you have two independent clauses joined together with a coordinating conjunction, you need to separate them with a comma. "Tim went to the store, and Beth went home."

There are some artistic exceptions to these rules, such as adding a pause for literary effect, but for the most part they are set in stone.

Commas are also used to separate items in a list. This area of English is unfortunately less clear than it should be, with two separate rules depending on what standard you are following. To understand the two different rules, let's pretend you are having a party at your house, and you are making a list of refreshments your friends will want. You may decide to serve three things: 1) pizza 2) chips 3) drinks. There are two different rules governing how you should punctuate this. According to many grammar books, you would write this as, "At the store I will buy pizza, chips, and drinks." This

variation puts a comma after each item in the list. It is the version that the style books used in most college English and history courses will prefer, so it is probably the one you should follow. However, the Associated Press style guide, which is used in college journalism classes and at newspapers and magazines, says the sentence should be written like this: "At the store I will buy pizza, chips and drinks." Here you only use a comma between the first two words, letting the word "and" act as the separator between the last two.

Another important place to use commas is when you have a modifier that describes an element of a sentence, but that does not directly follow the thing it describes. Look at the sentence: "Tim went over to visit Beth, watching the full moon along the way." In this sentence there is no confusion about who is "watching the full moon"; it is Tim, probably as he walks to Beth's house. If you remove the comma, however, you get this: "Tim went over to visit Beth watching the full moon along the way." Now it sounds as though Beth is watching the full moon, and we are forced to wonder what "way" the moon is traveling along.

Commas are also used when adding introductory prepositional phrases and introductory adverbs to sentences. A comma is always needed following an introductory adverb. ("Quickly, Jody ran to the car.") Commas are even necessary when you have an adverb introducing a clause within a sentence, even if the clause not the first clause of the sentence. ("Amanda wanted to go to the movie; however, she knew her homework was more important.")

With introductory prepositional phrases you only add a comma if the phrase (or if a group of introductory phrases) is five or more words long. Thus, the sentence you just read did not have a comma following its introductory prepositional phrase ("With introductory prepositional phrases") because it was only four words. Compare that to this sentence with a five word introductory phrase: "After the ridiculously long class, the friends needed to relax."

The last main way that commas are used in sentences is to separate out information that does not need to be there. For instance, "My cousin Hector, who wore a blue hat at the party, thought you were funny." The fact that Hector wore a blue hat is interesting, but it is not vital to the sentence; it could be removed and not changed the sentence's meaning. For that reason it gets commas around it. Along these lines you should remember that any clause introduced by the word that is considered to provide essential information to the sentence and should not get commas around it. Conversely, any clause starting with the word which is considered nonessential and should not get commas around it.

Quotation Marks

Quotation marks are used in English in a variety of different ways. The most common use of quotation marks is to show quotations either as dialogue or when directly quoting a source in an essay or news article. Fortunately, both of these uses follow the same basic rules.

When you have a quote written as the second part of a sentence, you need to put a comma before the quotation marks and a period inside the quotation marks at the end. (Franklin said, "Let's go to the store.") Conversely, when you have quote as the first part of the sentence with information describing it second, a comma replaces the period at the end of the sentence inside the quotes. ("Let's go to the store," Franklin said.)

If the information in a quote is not a complete sentence you do not need to capitalize it or put commas around it, provided that it is not dialogue. (No one thought the idea of "going to the store" sounded very fun.)

It is important to note that when the last word in a sentence has both a quotation mark and a period attached to it, the period is always inside the quotes. This is the case when you have a complete sentence inside a quote ("Let's go to the store."), and when the last word in a sentence just happens to have quote marks around it (Kerri said I was "mean.") You also need to do the same thing with commas. (Kerri said I was "mean," and it made me feel bad.) However, other punctuation marks such as colons, semicolons and dashes do not follow this rule and should come outside of the quotes. (Kerri said I was "mean"; it made me feel bad.)

When you want to use a quote inside a quote, you use the standard double-quotation marks for the outer quote and single-quotation marks for the inner quote. ("The sign on the door said 'no soliciting,' so we went to the next house.")

Non-period end punctuation marks—exclamation points and question marks—will sometimes go inside the quotation marks and sometimes outside, depending on how much of the sentence they refer to. If the end punctuation refers only to what is in the quote, it goes inside the quotation marks. ("Everyone fleeing the zombie attack screamed, "Run!") Quotation marks are also used around certain types of titles. To figure out which ones, it helps to look at which titles are not put in quotes as well.

Titles are generally broken down into two categories: large works and small works. Large works are things such as newspapers, magazines, CDs, books and television shows. The defining characteristic of a large work is that it is able to hold small works in it. Small works are the articles inside newspapers and magazines, the songs on a CD, the chapters in a book and the episodes of a television show. It is small works that get quotation marks around them. (Large works, meanwhile, are either underlined or italicized.)

Using quotation marks correctly in a title looks something like this: The two-page article entitled "San Francisco Giants Win World Series" appeared in yesterday's New York Times. The article title is in quotes, and the newspaper title is in italics.

How to Answer English Grammar Multiple Choice - Verb Tense

This tutorial is designed to help you answer English Grammar multiple choice questions as well as a very quick refresher on verb tenses. It is assumed that you have some familiarity with the verb tenses covered here. If you find these questions difficulty or do not understand the tense construction, we recommend you seek out additional instruction.

Tenses Covered

1. Past Progressive
2. Present Perfect
3. Present Perfect Progressive
4. Present Progressive
5. Simple Future
6. Simple Future – "Going to" Form
7. Past Perfect Progressive
8. Future Perfect Progressive
9. Future Perfect
10. Future Progressive
11. Past Perfect

1. The Past Progressive Tense

How to Recognize This Tense

He *was running* very fast when he fell.

They *were drinking* coffee when he arrived.

About the Past Progressive Tense

This tense is used to speak of an action that was in progress in the past when another event occurred.

The action was unfolding at a point in the past.

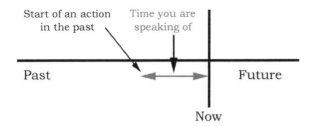

Past Progressive Tense Construction

This tense is formed by using the past tense of the verb "to be" plus the present participle of the main verb.

Sample Question

Bill _____ lunch when we arrived.

    a. will eat

    b. is eating

    c. eats

    d. was eating

How to Answer This Type of Question

1. First examine the question for clues about the time frame.

The sentence ends with "when we arrived," so we know the time frame is a point ("when") in the past (arrived).

The correct answer will refer to an ongoing action at a point of time in the past.

2. Examine the choices and eliminate any obviously incorrect answers.

Choice A is the future tense so we can eliminate.

Choice B is the present continuous so we can eliminate.

Choice C is present tense so we can eliminate.

Choice D refers to an action that takes place at a point of time in the past ("was eating").

2. The Present Perfect Tense

How to Recognize This Tense

I *have had* enough to eat.

We *have been* to Paris many times.

I *have known* him for five years.

I *have been* coming here since I was a child.

About the Present Perfect Tense

This tense expresses the idea that something happened (or didn't happen) at an unspecific time in the past until the present. The action happened at an unspecified time in the past. (If there is a specific time mentioned, the simple past tense is used.) It can be used for repeated action, accomplishments, changes over time and uncompleted action.

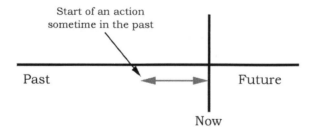

Present Perfect Tense Construction

It is also used with "for" and "since."

This tense is formed by using the present tense of the verb "to have" plus the past participle of the main verb.

Sample Question

I _____ these birds many times.

    a. am seeing

    b. will saw

    c. have seen

    d. have saw

How to Answer This Type of Question

1. First examine the question for clues about the time frame.

"Many times" tells us that the action is repeated and in the past.

2. Examine the choices and eliminate any obviously incorrect answers.

Choice A, "am seeing" is incorrect because it is a continuing action, i.e. in the present; it also doesn't use a form of 'have'.

Choice B is grammatically incorrect.

Choice C is tells of something that has happened in the past and is now over. This is the best choice so far.

Choice D is grammatically incorrect.

3. The Present Perfect Progressive Tense

How to Recognize This Tense

We *have been seeing* a lot of rainy days.

I *have been reading* some very good books.

About the Present Perfect Progressive Tense

This tense expresses the idea that something happened (or didn't happen) in the relatively recent past, but <u>the action is not finished.</u> It is used to express the duration of the action.

NOTE: The present perfect speaks of an action that happened sometime in the past, but this action is finished. In the present perfect progressive tense, the action that started in the past is still going on.

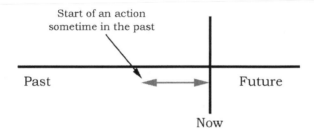

Present Perfect Progressive Tense Construction

This tense is formed by using the present tense of the verb "to have," plus "been," plus the present participle of the main verb.

Sample Question

Bill _____ there for two hours.

    a. sits

    b. sitting

    c. has been sitting

    d. will sat

How to Answer This Type of Question

1. First examine the question for clues about the time frame.

"For two hours" tells us that the action, "sits," is continuous up to now, and may continue into the future.

Note this sentence could also be the simple past tense,

Bill sat there for two hours.

Or the future tense,

Bill will sit there for two hours.

However, these are not among the choices.

2. Examine the choices and eliminate any obviously incorrect answers.

Choice A is incorrect because it is the present tense.
Choice B is incorrect because it is the present continuous.
Choice C is correct. "Has been sitting" expresses a continuous action in the past that isn't finished.
Choice D is grammatically incorrect.

4. The Present Progressive Tense

How to Recognize This Tense

We *are having* a delicious lunch.

They *are driving* much too fast.

About the Present Progressive Tense

This tense is used to express what the action is <u>right now</u>. The action started in the recent past, and is continuing into the future.

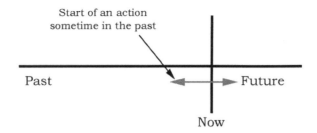

Start of an action
sometime in the past

Past   Future

Now

Present Perfect Tense Construction

The Present Progressive Tense is formed by using the present tense of "to be" plus the present participle of the main verb.

Sample Question

She _____ very hard these days.

    a. works

    b. is working

    c. will work

    d. worked

How to Answer This Type of Question

1. First examine the question for clues about the time frame.

The end of the sentence includes "these days" which tell us the action started in the past, continues into the present, and may continue into the future.

2. Examine the choices and eliminate any obviously incorrect answers.

Choice A, the simple present is incorrect.
Choice B, "is working" is correct.
Check the other two choices just to be sure. Choice C is fu-

ture tense, and choice D is past tense, so they can be eliminated.

The correct answer is choice B.

5. The Simple Future Tense

How to Recognize This Tense

I *will see* you tomorrow.
We *will drive* the car.

About the Simple Future Tense

This tense shows that the action will happen sometime in the future.

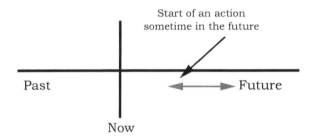

Simple Future Tense Construction

The tense is formed by using "will" plus the root form of the verb. (The root form of the verb is the infinitive without "to." Examples: read, swim.)

Sample Question

We _____ to Paris next year.

   a. went

   b. had been

   c. will go

   d. go

How to Answer This Type of Question

1. First examine the question for clues about the time frame.

The last two words of the sentence, "next year," clearly identify this sentence as referring to the future.

2. Examine the choices and eliminate any obviously incorrect answers.

Choice A is the past tense and can be eliminated.

Choice B is the past perfect tense and can be eliminated.

Choice D is the simple present and can be eliminated.

Choice C is the only one left and is the correct simple future tense.

6. The Simple Future Tense – The "Going to" Form

How to Recognize This Tense

I *am going to* see you tomorrow.

We *are going to* drive the car.

About the Simple Future Tense

This form of the future tense is used to show the intention of doing something in the future. (This is the strict grammatical meaning, but in daily speech, it is often used interchangeably with the simple future tense, the "will" form.)

The tense is formed by using the present conditional tense of "to go," plus the infinitive of the verb.

Sample Question

I _____ shopping in an hour.

    a. go

    b. have gone

    c. am going to go

    d. went

How to Answer This Type of Question

1. First examine the question for clues about the time frame.

"In an hour" clearly identifies the action as taking place in the future.

2. Examine the choices and eliminate any obviously incorrect answers.

Choice A is the simple present tense and can also be eliminated.

Choice B is the past perfect and can be eliminated.

Choice C is the correct answer.

Choice D is the past tense and can be eliminated.

7. The Past Perfect Progressive Tense

How to Recognize This Tense

I *had been sleeping* for an hour when you phoned.

We *had been eating* our dinner when they all came into the dining room.

About the Past Perfect Progressive Tense

This tense is used to show that the action had been going on for a period of time in the past when another action, also in the past, occurred.

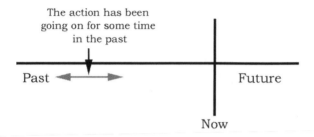

The action has been
going on for some time
in the past

Past ◄──────► Future

Now

Past Perfect Tense Construction

The tense is formed by using the past perfect tense of the verb "to be" plus the present participle of the main verb.

Sample Question

How long _____ you _____ when I saw you?

    a. are _____ running

    b. had _____ running

    c. had _____ been running

    d. was _____ running

How to Answer This Type of Question

1. First examine the question for clues about the time frame.

"When I saw" tells us the sentence happened at a point of time ("when") in the past ("saw").

2. Examine the choices and eliminate any obviously incorrect answers.

Choice A, "are running" is incorrect and can be eliminated.

Choice B, "Had ___ running" is grammatically incorrect and can be eliminated.

Choice C is correct.

Choice D is grammatically incorrect so the answer is choice C.

8. Future Perfect Progressive Tense

How to Recognize This Tense

I *will have been working* here for two years in March.

I *will have been driving* for four hours when I get there, so I will be tired.

About the Future Perfect Progressive Tense

This tense is used to show that the action continues up to a point of time in the future.

Future Prefect Progressive Tense Construction

This tense is formed by using the future perfect tense of "to be" plus the present participle of the main verb.

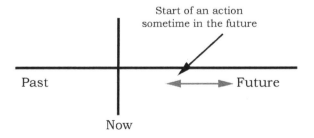

Sample Question

_____ you _____ all the time
I am gone?

    a. have _____ been working

    b. will _____ have been working

    c. are _____ worked

    d. will _____ worked

How to Answer This Type of Question

1. First examine the question for clues about the time frame.

"All the time I am gone" refers to an action in the future ("time I am gone") and the action is progressive ("all the time"). The progressive action means the correct choice will be a verb tense that ends in "ing."

2. Examine the choices and eliminate any obviously incorrect answers.

Choice A, the past perfect, refers to a past continuous event and is also grammatically incorrect in the sentence, so choice A can be eliminated.

Choice B looks correct because it refers to an action will be going on for a period of time in the future.

Examine choices C and D just to be sure. Both choices are grammatically incorrect and can be eliminated. Choice B is the correct answer.

9. The Future Perfect Tense

How to Recognize This Tense

By next November, I *will have received* my promotion.

By the time he gets home, she is going *to have cleaned* the entire house.

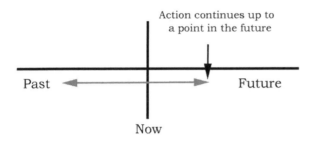

About the Future Perfect Tense

The future perfect tense expresses action in the future before another action in the future. This is the past in the future. For example:

He *will have prepared* dinner when she arrives.

Future Perfect Tense Construction

This tense is formed by "will + have + past participle."

Sample Question

They _____ their seats before the game begins.

    a. will have find

    b. will find

    c. will have found

    d. found

How to Answer This Type of Question

1. First examine the question for clues about the time frame.

This question could be several different tenses. The only clue about the time frame is "before the game begins," which refers to a specific point of time.

We know it isn't in the past, because "begins" is incorrect for the past tense. Similarly with the present. So the question is about something that happens in the future, before another event in the future.

2. Examine the choices and eliminate any obviously incorrect answers.

Choice A can be eliminated as incorrect. Choice B looks good, so mark it and check the others before making a final decision. Choice C is the past perfect and can be eliminated because the time frame is incorrect. Choice D is the simple past tense and can be eliminated for the same reason.

10. Future Progressive Tense

How to Recognize This Tense

The teams *will be playing* soccer when we arrive.

At 3:45 the soccer fans *will be waiting* for the game to start at 4:00 o'clock

At 3:45 the soccer players *will be preparing* to play at 4:00 o'clock

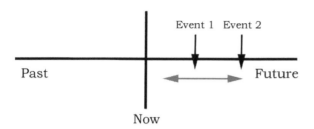

About the Future Progressive Tense

The future progressive tense talks about a continuing action in the future.

Future Progressive Tense Construction

will+ be + (root form) + ing = will be playing

Sample Question

Many excited fans _____ a bus to see the game at 4:00.

    a. catch

    b. catching

    c. have been catching

    d. will be catching

How to Answer This Type of Question

1. First examine the question for clues about the time frame.

"At 4:00," tells us the sentence is either in the past OR in the future.

2. Examine the choices and eliminate any obviously incorrect answers.

From the time frame of the sentence, the answer will be past or future tense.

Choice A is the present tense and can be eliminated. Choice B is the present continuous tense and can be eliminated. Choice C is the past perfect continuous and can be eliminated. Choice D is the only one left. Quickly examining the tense, it is future progressive and is correct in the sentence.

11. The Past Perfect Tense

How to Recognize This Tense

The party *had* just *started* when the coach arrived.

We *had waited* for twenty minutes when the bus finally came.

About the Past Perfect

The past perfect tense talks about two events that happened in the past and establishes which event happened first.

Another example is, "We had eaten when he arrived."

The two events are "eat" and "he arrived." From the sentence above the past perfect tense tells us the first event, "eat" happened before the second event, "he arrived."

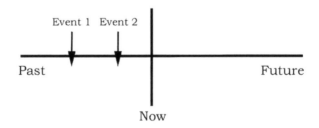

I had already eaten when my friends arrived.

Past Perfect Tense Construction

The past perfect is formed by "have" plus the past participle.

Sample Question

It was time to go home after they _____ the game.

    a. will win

    b. win

    c. had won

    d. wins

How to Answer This Type of Question

1. First examine the question for clues about the time frame.

"Was" tells us the sentence happened in the past. Also notice there are two events, "go home" and "after the game."

2. Examine the choices and eliminate any obviously incorrect answers.

Choice A is the future tense and can be eliminated. Choice B is the simple present and can be eliminated. Choice C is the past perfect and orders the two events in the past. Choice D is the present tense and incorrect and can be eliminated, so choice C is the correct answer.

How to Write an Essay

Writing an essay can be a difficult process, especially if you are under time constraints such as during an exam. Here are three simple steps to help you to write a solid, well thought out essay:

1. **Brainstorm** potential themes and general ideas for your essay.

2. **Outline** your essay step by step, including subheadings for ease of understanding.

3. **Write** your essay carefully being aware of proper grammar and sentence structure.

1. Brainstorming

You should first spend some time thinking about the general subject of the essay. If the essay is asking a question, you must make sure to answer this fully in your essay. You may find it helpful to highlight key words in your assignment or use a simple spider diagram to jot down key ideas.

Example

> Read the following information and complete the following assignment:
>
> Joseph Conrad is a Polish author who lived in England for most of his life and wrote a prolific amount of English literature. Much of his work was completed during the height of the British Empire's colonial imperialism.
>
> Assignment: What impact has Joseph Conrad had on modern society? Present your point of view on the matter and support it with evidence. Your evidence may include reasoning, logic, examples from readings, your

own experience, and observations.

Joseph Conrad

Background? sailor, adventure, Polish immigrant, Youth, Nostromo, Heart of Darkness
Themes in his works? ivory, silver trading, colonialism, corruption, greed
Thoughts? descent into madness, nature of evil

2. Outlining (or planning)

An outline or plan is critical to organize your thoughts and ideas fully and logically. There are many ways to do this; the easiest is to write down the following headings:

1. Title
2. Introduction
3. Body
4. Conclusion

You should then jot down key ideas and themes that fit logically under the appropriate heading. This plan is now the backbone of your essay.

Tip: Even if you are not required to produce an outline or plan for the assignment, you should always leave it with your essay in the exam booklet or the back of the assignment paper. Simply draw a line across it and write 'plan' or 'outline'. This demonstrates to the reader the approach you use in formulating and finally writing your essay.

3. Writing the essay

Your introduction is what will help the reader to decide whether they want to read the rest of your essay. The introduction also introduces the subject matter and allows you to provide a general background to the reader. The first sentence is very important and you should avoid starting the essay with openers such as 'I will be comparing...'

Example

> Born as Józef Teodor Konrad Korzeniowski on December 3rd, 1857, Joseph Conrad led an adventurous life. As a Polish immigrant, Conrad never quite fit into England where he spent most of his adult life. As a younger man, Conrad made a living off sailing voyages. These swashbuckling experiences soon had him writing tales of the high seas such as one of his first works, Youth. While his early, adventurous work was of high quality, Conrad is best remembered for shedding light on the exploitative side of colonialism. Age and experience led him to start writing about (and challenging) the darker side of the imperial way of thinking. Conrad's work has forever soured words such as colonialism and imperialism.

In the main part, or body of your essay, you should always be yourself and be original.

- Avoid using clichés.
- Be aware of your tone.
- Consider the language that you use. Avoid jargon and slang. Use clear prose and imagery.
- Your writing should always flow; remember to use transitions, especially between paragraphs. Read aloud in your head to make sure a paragraph sounds right.
- Always try to use a new paragraph for new ideas.

Example

> *Conrad's written fiction focused on themes such as greed and power. He portrayed these two concepts as purveyors of evil. Greed and power may take on different guises, but the end result would always be the same.*

Perhaps his most famous piece, The Heart of
Darkness, is about the descent of an English
ivory trader, Mr. Kurtz, into madness. We are
taken up a river resembling the Congo by a
narrator, Marlow, who is sent to retrieve Mr.
Kurtz. Marlow eventually finds that Kurtz
has been diluted by power and greed, the
two things that spurred on colonialism in
Africa. Kurtz has taken charge of a large tribe
of natives (that he brutalizes) and has been
hoarding ivory for himself.

Much of Conrad's later work was cut from
the same vein as The Heart of Darkness. His
crowning achievement is considered Nostromo
where he takes an idealistic hero and corrupts
him with colonial greed. Only this time the
greed is for silver, not ivory.

Conrad's work resonates with readers partly
because it was semi-autobiographical. Where
his experience sailing the high seas helped
bring his adventure stories to light, likewise
did his experience witnessing atrocities in
Africa reverberate through his writing.

The conclusion is your last chance to impress your reader
and brings your entire essay to a logical close. You may want
to link your conclusion back to your introduction or provide
some closing statements. Do not panic if you cannot close
your essay off completely. Few subjects offer closure.

Your conclusion should always be consistent with the rest of
the essay and you should never introduce a new idea in your
conclusion. It is also important to remember that a weak
conclusion can diminish the impact of a good essay.

Example

In sum, Joseph Conrad's life experiences and
masterful writing left a lasting impact on the

image of progress and what it meant to "move forward." He brought to light the cost in human lives that was required for Europe to continue mining natural resources from foreign lands. Joseph Conrad had a permanent impact on imperial culture, and colonial brutality has been on the decline ever since his work was published.

Presentation

Poor grammar and punctuation can ruin an otherwise good essay. You should always follow any requirements about the presentation of your essay, such as word count. You should also make sure that your writing is legible. Always allow time for one final read-through before submission.

Tip: If you are able to, write with double spacing. If you make a mistake, you can cross it out and write the correction on the blank line above.

Some final points to think about for writing a solid, well thought out essay:

- A good essay will contain a strong focus.

- There is no set essay structure but you can use sub-headings for better readability.

- Avoid particularly sensitive or controversial material. If you must write about something controversial, always make sure to include counter arguments.

- Your essay may have little to do with the subject itself; it is about what you make of the subject.

- Your essay can include examples from your readings, experience, studies or observations.

- Spend time doing practice essays and looking at sample essays beforehand.

Another Example

Lets look at another example using the three steps required to write a good essay:

1. **Brainstorming**

2. **Outlining**

3. **Writing**

Using a second essay, we can now explore these three steps in further detail.

1. Brainstorming

Example

> Think about the information that follows and the assignment below.
>
> People often quote the last two lines of Robert Frost's "The Road not Taken" as being metaphorical for success. The line's read "I took the one less travelled by, / And that has made all the difference" (19, 20).
>
> Assignment: Analyze and interpret this poem. Consider the poem's place in Modernist culture and Robert Frost's personal experiences. Read in between the lines and identify the more complex aspects/themes of this poem. Outline and complete an essay that challenges the point of view presented above, that the poem is synonymous with success. Provide evidence backed up by logic, experience, research, and/ or examples from the poem.

The assignment and key words that appear in the brief above are being highlighted. This confirms that the essay is not asking a specific question, but instead, it is asking for discussion of the subject matter and phrases.
This is the time to take a few moments to jot down initial

thoughts about the assignment. Do not worry too much about proper grammar at this point, just get all your thoughts down on paper:
"The Road Not Taken" by Robert Frost

> **Background?** Modernist poetry
> **Themes?** Life decisions, regret, fate, the unknown future
> **Thoughts?** The diverging roads are symbolic, the sigh at end signifies regret, life has many twists and turns, you can end in a drastically different situation later after a simple decision now

2. Outlining (or Planning)

Outlining or planning is the next important stage in the process and you should always spend a few minutes writing a plan. This plan is just as important as the essay itself. You can also note how much **time** you may want to spend on a particular section. Make sure to assign headings to each main section of the essay and include important questions/ themes you want to address.

Example

> **1. Title**
>
> **2. Essay introduction**
> *Identify and discuss the underlying theme/s in Robert Frost's "The Road Not Taken"*
> *What was Frost's background and its applicability to understanding this poem?*
>
> **3. Essay body**
> *Quick summary of the poem*
> *Discuss key themes and other concepts*
> *Discuss how these things relate to Modernism*
>
> **4. Essay conclusion**
> *Rephrase the themes of Robert Frost's poem and their place in modernist doctrine*

This plan is now the outline for the essay.

3. Writing

The introduction is important, as it needs to introduce the reader to the essay in a way that will encourage them to continue reading. A good introduction will introduce the subject matter to a reader and point out relevant information that may be helpful to know when reading the rest of the essay.

Example

> Identify and discuss the underlying theme/s in Robert Frost's "The Road Not Taken"
>
> *Robert Frost wrote during the artistic movement after World War I known as Modernism. One purpose of modernism was to remake things in a new light, to analyze and change symptoms of societies that had plunged the European world into a grisly war. Frost's poem, "The Road Not Taken," carries with it a burden of regret that was a staple of Modernist art.*

This introduction opens with what explaining about the time period of Robert Frost and real life influences to the theme of his poem, "The Road Not Taken." It contains some powerful language that will encourage the reader to continue reading and gives a solid base in understanding the remainder of the essay.

The main part or **body of the essay** is also very important:

Example

> *"The Road Not Taken" was almost assuredly influenced by Robert Frost's personal life. He was very familiar with facing difficult decisions. Frost had to make the decision to send both his sister and daughter to mental institutions. His son Carol committed suicide at the age of 38. The list of loss Frost experienced in his life goes on, but it suffices to say he was familiar with questioning the past.*

With no other hints of the narrator's identity, it is best to assume that he is a man similar to Frost himself. The poem itself is about a nameless narrator reflecting on when he travelled through the autumn woods one day. He had come across a split in the road and expresses regret that he could not travel both. Each road is described as looking similar and as having equal wear but it is also mentioned one was grassier. The roads were unknown to the narrator, and shared equal possibilities in how well they may or may not be around their bends. He tells his listener with a sigh that he had made his decision and had taken "the road less travelled by" (19). Even though he had little idea which road would be better in the long run, the one he chose proved difficult.

This poem is a collection of all the insecurities and possibilities that come with even the simplest decisions. We experience the sorrow expressed by the narrator in the opening lines with every decision we make. For all the choices you make in life, there is a counterweight of choices you have not made. In a way, we are all missing half of our lives' possibilities. This realization causes a mixture of regret and nostalgia, but also stokes in us the keen awareness that missed opportunities are inevitable and regretting them is a waste of energy. We often find ourselves stuck, as the narrator is, between questioning the decisions we've made and knowing that this natural process isn't exactly productive.

Unsolvable regret and nostalgia are things that the Modernists fought with on a regular basis. They often experimented in taking happenings of the past and reinventing them to fit a new future.

The body of the essay opens with providing a brief overview of Robert Frost's personal life and his life's relevance to the over arching theme of dealing with difficult decisions in the poem, "The Road Not Taken."

A new paragraph starts where appropriate and at the end of the discussion of Robert Frost's life, a **transition** moves the reader back to the start of the book (closing off this section). This also helps to move the reader towards the next discussion point.

The tone of this essay is formal, mainly because of the seriousness of the subject – regret and nostalgia plays a major role in people's lives all around the world.

For the conclusion, there will be a summary of the main discussion. While it is ideal for you to impress the reader with your writing, more importantly you need to make sure you cover all your bases and address the assignment appropriately with a closing statement about any important points you discussed in the body of your essay.

Example

> *In conclusion, Robert Frost's poem "The Road Not Taken" deals with themes of fate, regret, sorrow, and the many possibilities our decisions hold. Consider how easy it would be to upturn your life today if you made a few decisions you normally wouldn't. Frost's poem forces us to consider the twists and turns our lives take. Perhaps with a sigh, we could all think about the choices that for us have made all the difference.*

This conclusion is consistent with the rest of the essay in terms of style. There are no new ideas introduced and it has referred to the main points in the assignment title.

Finally, a full read-through is necessary before submission. It only takes a couple of minutes to read through and pick up any errors. Remember to double space to leave room for any corrections to be made. You can also leave spacing at the end of each paragraph if you should need to add an additional sentence or two.

Common Essay Mistakes - Example 1

Whether the topic is love or action, reality television shows damage society. Viewers witness the personal struggles of strangers and they experience an outpouring of emotions in the name of entertainment. This can be dangerous on many levels. Viewers become numb to real emotions and values. Run the risk of not interpreting a dangerous situation correctly. 1 The reality show participant is also at risk because they are completely exposed. 2 The damage to both viewers and participants leads to the destruction of our healthy societal values.

Romance reality shows are dangerous to the participants and contribute to the emotional problems witnessed in society today as we set up a system built on equality and respect, shows like "The Bachelor" tear it down. 3 In front of millions of viewers every week, young women compete for a man. Twenty-five women claim to be in love with a man they just met. The man is reduced to an object they compete for. There are tears, fights, and manipulation aimed at winning the prize. 4 Imagine a young woman's reality when she returns home and faces the scrutiny of viewers who watched her unravel on television every Monday night. These women objectify themselves and have learned 5 that relationships are a combination of hysteria and competition. This does not give hope to a society based on family values and equality.

6 While incorporating the same manipulations and breakdown of relationships offered on "The Bachelor," shows like "Survivor" add another level of danger. Not only are they building a society based on lying to each other, they are competing in physical challenges that become dangerous. In the name of entertainment, these challenges become increasingly physical and are usually held in a hostile environment. The viewer's ability to determine the safety of an activity is messed up. 7 To entertain and preserve their pride, participants continue in competitions regardless of the danger level. For example, 8 participants on "Survivor" have sustained serious injuries as heart attack and burns.

Societal rules are based on the safety of its citizens, not on hurting yourself for entertainment.

Reality shows of all kinds are dangerous to participants. They damage society. 9

1. Correct sentence fragments. Who/what runs the risk? Add a subject or combine sentences. Try: "Viewers become numb to real emotions and run the risk of not interpreting a dangerous situation correctly."

2. Correct redundant phrases. Try: "The reality show participant is also at risk because they are exposed."

3. Correct run-on sentences. Decide which thoughts should be separated. Try: "Romance reality shows are dangerous to participants and contribute to the emotional problems of society today. As we support a system built on equality and respect, shows like "The Bachelor" tear it down."

4. Vary sentence structure and length. Try: "Twenty-five women claim to be in love with a man who is reduced to being the object of competition. There are tears, fights, and manipulation aimed at winning the prize."

5. Use active voice. Try: These women objectify themselves and learned that relationships are a combination of hysteria and competition.

6. Use transitions to tie paragraphs together. Try: Start the paragraph with, "Action oriented reality shows are equally as dangerous to the participants."

7. Avoid casual language/slang. Try: "The viewer's ability to determine the safety of an activity is compromised."

8. Don't address the essay. Avoid phrases like "for example" and "in conclusion." Try: "Participants on "Survivor" have sustained serious injuries as heart attack and burns.

9. Leave yourself time to write a strong conclusion! Try: Designate 3-5 minutes for writing your conclusion.

Common Essay Mistakes - Example 2

Questioning authority makes society stronger. In every aspect our society, there is an authoritative person or group making rules. There is also the group underneath them who are meant to follow. 1 This is true of our country's public schools as well as our federal government. The right to question authority at both of these levels is guaranteed by the United States Declaration of Independence. People are given the ability to question so that authority figures are kept in check 2 and will be forced to listen to the opinions of other people. Questioning authority leads to positive changes in society and preserves what is already working well.

If students never question the authority of a principal's decisions, the best interest of the student body is lost. Good things 3 may not remain in place for the students and no amendment to the rules are sought. Change requires that authority be questioned. For example, that Silver Head Middle School in Davie, Florida. Last year, the principal felt strongly about enforcing the school's uniform policy. Some students were not bothered by this. 4 Many students felt the policy disregarded their civil rights. A petition voicing student dissatisfaction was signed and presented to the principal. He met with a student representative to discuss the petition. Compromise was reached as a monthly "casual day." The students were able to promote change and peace by questioning authority.

Even at the level of federal government, our country's ultimate authority, the ability to question is the key to the harmony keeping society strong. Most government officials are elected by the public so they have the right to question their authority. 5 If there's a mandate, law, or statement that citizens aren't 6 happy with, they have recourse. Campaigning for, or against a political platform and participating in the electoral process give a voice to every opinion. I think elections are very important. 7 Without this questioning and examination of society's laws, the government will represent only the voice of the authority figure. The success of our society is based on the questioning of authority. 8

Society is strengthened by those who question authority. Dialogue is created between people with different visions and change becomes possible. At both the level of public school and of federal government, the positive effects of questioning authority can be witnessed. Whether questioning the decisions of a single principal or the motives of the federal government, it is the willingness of people to question and create change that allows society to grow. A strong society is inspired by many voices, all at different levels. 9 These voices keep society strong.

1. Write concisely. Combine the sentences to improve understanding and cut unnecessary words. Try: "In every aspect of society, there is an authority making rules and a group of people meant to follow them."

2. Avoid slang. Re-word "kept in check." Try: "People are given the ability to question so that authority figures are held accountable and will be forced to listen to the opinions of other people.

2-2. Cut unnecessary words. Try: "People are given the ability to question so that authority figures are held accountable and will listen to other opinions."

3. Use precise language. What are "good things?" Try: "Interesting activities may not remain in place for the students and no amendment to the rules are sought."

Use correct subject-verb agreement. Be careful to identify the correct subject of your sentence. Try: "Interesting activities may not remain in place for the students and no amendment to the rules is sought."

4. Don't add information that doesn't add value to your argument. Cut: "Some students weren't bothered by this."

5. Check for parallel structure. Who has the right to question whose authority? Try: "Having voted them in, the people have the authority to question public officials."

6. Don't use contractions in academic essays. Try: "If there is a mandate, law, or statement that citizens are not happy with, they have recourse."

7. Don't use the pronoun "I" in persuasive essays. Cut opinions. Cut:"I think elections are very important."

8. Use specific examples to prove your argument. Try: Discuss a particular election in depth.

9. Cut redundant sentences. Cut: "A strong society is inspired by many voices, all at different levels."

Writing Concisely

Concise writing is direct and descriptive. The reader follows the writer's thoughts easily. If your writing is concise, a four paragraph essay is acceptable for standardized tests. It's better to write clearly about fewer ideas than to write poorly about many.

This doesn't always mean using fewer words. It means that every word you use is important to the message. Unnecessary or repetitive information dilutes ideas and weakens your writing. The meaning of the word concise comes from the Latin, "to cut up." If it isn't necessary information, don't waste precious testing minutes writing it down.

Being redundant is a quick way to lengthen a sentence or paragraph, but it takes away your power during a timed essay. While many writers use repetition of phrases and key words to make their point, it's important to remove words that don't add value. Redundancy can confuse and lead you away from your subject when you need to write quickly. Be aware that many redundant phrases are part of our daily language and need to be cut from your essay.

For example, "bouquet of flowers" is a redundant phrase as only the word "bouquet" is necessary. Its definition includes flowers. Be especially careful with words you use to stress a point, such as "completely," "totally," and "very."

First of all, I'd like to thank my family.
Revised: First, I'd like to thank my family.

The school *introduced a new* rule.
Revised: The school introduced a rule.

I am *completely full.*
Revised: I am full.

Your glass is *totally empty*!
Revised: Your glass is empty!

Her artwork is *very unique.*
Revised: Her artwork is unique.

Other ways to cut bulk and time include avoiding phrases that have no meaning or power in your essay. Phrases like "in my opinion," "as a matter of fact," and "due to the fact that" are space and time wasters. Also, change passive verbs to active voice.

In my opinion, the paper is well written.
Revised: The paper is well written.

The book *was written* by the best students.
Revised: The best students wrote the book.

The teacher *is listening* to the students.
The teacher listens to the students.

This assigns action to the subject, shortens, and clarifies the sentence. When time is working against you, precise language is on your side.

Not only should you remove redundant phrases, whole sentences without value should be cut too. Replacing general nouns with specific ones is an effective way to accomplish this.

She screamed as the thing came closer. It was a sharp-toothed dog.
Revised: She screamed as the sharp-toothed dog came closer.

The revised sentence is precise and the paragraph is improved by combining sentences and varying sentence structure. When editing, ask yourself which thoughts should be connected and which need to be separated. Skim each paragraph as you finish writing it and cut as you go.

Leave three to four minutes for final editing. While reading, make a point to pause at every period. This allows you to "hear" sentences the way your reader will, not how you meant them to sound. This will help you find the phrases and sentences that need to be cut or combined. The result is an essay a grader will appreciate.

Avoiding Redundancy

Duplication and verbosity in English is the use of two or more words that clearly mean the same thing, making one of them unnecessary. It is easy to do use redundant expressions or phrases in a conversation where speech is spontaneous, and common in spoken English. In written English, however, redundancy is more serious and harder to ignore. Here are list of redundant phrases to avoid.

1. Suddenly exploded.

An explosion is instantaneous or immediate and that is sudden enough. No need to use 'suddenly' along with exploded.

2. Final outcome.

An outcome refers to the result. An outcome is intrinsically final and so no need to use final along with outcome.

3. Advance notice/planning/reservations/ warning.

A warning, notice, reservation or plan is made before an event. Once the reader sees any of these words, they know that they were done or carried out before the event. These words do not need to be used with advance.

4. First began, new beginning.

Beginning signals the start or the first time, and therefore the use of "new" is superfluous.

5. Add an additional.

The word 'add' indicates the provision of another something, and so "additional" is superfluous.

6. For a period/number of days.

The word "days" is already in plural and clearly signifies more than just one day. It is thus redundant to use "a number of," or "a period of" along with days. Simply state the number of days or of the specific number of days is unknown, you say 'many days.'

7. Foreign imports.

Imports are foreign as they come from another country, so it is superfluous to refer to imports as "foreign."

8. Forever and ever.

Forever indicates eternity and so there is no need for "ever" as it simply duplicated forever.

9. Came at a time when.

"At a time" is not necessary in this phrase because the 'when' already provides a temporal reference to the action, coming.

10. Free gift.

It cannot be a gift if it is paid for. A gift, by nature, is free and so referring to a gift is free is redundant.

11. Collaborate/join/meet/merge together.

The words merge, join, meet and collaborate already suggest people or things coming together. It is unnecessary to use any of these words with together, such as saying merge together or join together. The correct expression is to simply say join or merge, omitting the together.

12. Invited guests.

Guests are those invited for an event. Since they had to be invited to be guests, there is no need to use invited with guests.

13. Major breakthrough.

A breakthrough is significant by nature. It can only be described as a breakthrough when there is a notable progress. The significant nature of the progress is already implied when you use the word "breakthrough," so "major" is redundant.

14. Absolutely certain or sure/essential/ guaranteed.

When someone or something is said to be sure or certain it indicates that it is without doubt. Using "absolutely" in addition to certain or sure is unnecessary. Essential or guaranteed is used for something that is absolute and so also does not need the word absolutely to accompany them.

15. Ask a question.

Ask means to present a question. Using "question" in addition to "ask" is redundant.

16. Basic fundamentals/essentials.

Using basic here is redundant. Essentials and fundamental suggest an elementary nature.

17. [Number] a.m. in the morning/p.m. in the evening.

When you write 8 a.m. the reader knows you mean 8 o'clock in the morning. It is not necessary to say 8 a.m. in the morning. Simply write 8 a.m. or 8 p.m.

18. Definite decision.

A decision is already definite even if it can be reversed later. A decision is a definite course of action has been chosen. No need to use the word definite along with the word decision.

19. Past history/record.

A record or history by definition refers to past events or occurrences. Using past to qualify history or record is unnecessary.

20. Consensus of opinion.

Consensus means agreement over something that may be or not be an opinion. So it may look that using the phrase 'consensus of opinion' is appropriate, but it is better to omit "opinion."

21. Enter in.

Enter means going in, as no one enters out. Therefore no need to add "in," simply use "enter."

22. Plan ahead.

You cannot plan for the past. Planning can only be done for the future. When you use "plan," the future is already implied.

23. Possibly might.

The words might and possibly signify probability, so just use one at a time.

24. Direct confrontation.

A confrontation is a head-on conflict, and does not need to be modified with "direct."

25. Postpone until later.

Something postponed is delayed or moved to a later time, and does not need to be modified with "later."

26. False pretense.

The word pretense is only used to describe a deception, so a "false" pretense is redundant.

27. Protest against.

Protest involves showing opposition; there is no need to use against.

28. End result.

Result only comes at the end. The reader who sees the word 'result' already knows that it occurs at the end.

29. Estimated at about/roughly.

Estimates are approximations that are not expected to be accurate, and do not need to be modified with "roughly" or "about."

30. Repeat again.

Repeat refers to something done again and does not need to be modified with "again."

31. Difficult dilemma.

A dilemma is a situation that is complicated or difficult, and does not need to be modified with "difficult."

32. Revert back.

Revert indicates returning to a former or earlier state. Something that reverts goes back to how it used to be. No need to add back.

33. (During the) course (of).

During means "in or throughout the duration of," and doesn't require the use of the word "course."

34. Same identical.

Same and identical means the same thing and should not be used together.

35. Completely filled/finished/opposite.

Completely indicates thoroughness. However, the words finished and filled already indicate something thoroughly filled or finished to the extent possible. The words filled and finished thus do not need to be qualified with "completely."

36. Since the time when.

In this phrase, 'the time when' is not necessary as 'since' already indicates sometime in the past.

37. Close proximity/scrutiny.

Proximity means being close, in respect to location. Scrutiny means studying something closely. Both words already suggest close, whether in respect to location as with proximity, or in respect to study, as with scrutiny. It is therefore unnecessary to use the words together.

38. Spell out in detail.

'Spell out' involves providing details, so no need to add "in detail."

39. Written down.

Anything written can be said to be taken down. Written should therefore be used on its own.

40. (Filled to) capacity.

Anything that is filled has reached its capacity and so the word capacity does not need to be used along with filled.

41. Unintended mistake.

Something is a mistake because it is not intended. The lack of intention is plain and so there is no need to qualify with "unintended."

42. Still remains.

"Remains" signifies that something is still as it is, and so using 'still' is superfluous.

43. Actual experience/fact.

Something becomes an experience after it has occurred. If it didn't occur it is not an experience. A fact can only be a fact when it is sure or confirmed. Both experience and fact thus do not need to be modified with "actual."

44. Therapeutic treatment.

Therapeutic refers to the healing or curing of illness. By nature all medical treatment is therapeutic in that it aims to heal or cure. When speaking of medical treatment, there is thus no need to use therapeutic to qualify treatment.

45. At the present time.

"At present" alone indicates the present time or "at this

time." Using "at the present time" is the verbose version. Better to just use "at present."

46. Unexpected surprise.

A surprise is unexpected by nature. The unexpected nature is assumed once the word surprised is read or heard. No need to use unexpected to qualify it.

47. As for example.

"As" indicates the use of an example and so it is redundant to say "an example."

48. Usual custom.

A custom refers to something that is observed or done repeatedly or routinely. The use of 'usual' along with custom is not necessary.

49. Added bonus.

Bonus already indicates something extra, in addition to the ordinary. Using "added" to describe the bonus is not necessary.

50. Few in number.

Something is few because it is small in number. No need to use number with few.

Practice Test Questions Set 1

T he questions below are not the same as you will find on the PERT - that would be too easy! And nobody knows what the questions will be and they change all the time. Below are general questions that cover the same subject areas as the PERT. So, while the format and exact wording of the questions may differ slightly, and change from year to year, if you can answer the questions below, you will have no problem with the PERT.

For the best results, take these practice test questions as if it were the real exam. Set aside time when you will not be disturbed, and a location that is quiet and free of distractions. Read the instructions carefully, read each question carefully, and answer to the best of your ability.
Use the bubble answer sheets provided. When you have completed the practice questions, check your answer against the Answer Key and read the explanation provided.

Do not attempt more than one set of practice test questions in one day. After completing the first practice test, wait two or three days before attempting the second set of questions.

Reading Answer Sheet

1. Ⓐ Ⓑ Ⓒ Ⓓ   11. Ⓐ Ⓑ Ⓒ Ⓓ   21. Ⓐ Ⓑ Ⓒ Ⓓ

2. Ⓐ Ⓑ Ⓒ Ⓓ   12. Ⓐ Ⓑ Ⓒ Ⓓ   22. Ⓐ Ⓑ Ⓒ Ⓓ

3. Ⓐ Ⓑ Ⓒ Ⓓ   13. Ⓐ Ⓑ Ⓒ Ⓓ   23. Ⓐ Ⓑ Ⓒ Ⓓ

4. Ⓐ Ⓑ Ⓒ Ⓓ   14. Ⓐ Ⓑ Ⓒ Ⓓ   24. Ⓐ Ⓑ Ⓒ Ⓓ

5. Ⓐ Ⓑ Ⓒ Ⓓ   15. Ⓐ Ⓑ Ⓒ Ⓓ   25. Ⓐ Ⓑ Ⓒ Ⓓ

6. Ⓐ Ⓑ Ⓒ Ⓓ   16. Ⓐ Ⓑ Ⓒ Ⓓ   26. Ⓐ Ⓑ Ⓒ Ⓓ

7. Ⓐ Ⓑ Ⓒ Ⓓ   17. Ⓐ Ⓑ Ⓒ Ⓓ   27. Ⓐ Ⓑ Ⓒ Ⓓ

8. Ⓐ Ⓑ Ⓒ Ⓓ   18. Ⓐ Ⓑ Ⓒ Ⓓ   28. Ⓐ Ⓑ Ⓒ Ⓓ

9. Ⓐ Ⓑ Ⓒ Ⓓ   19. Ⓐ Ⓑ Ⓒ Ⓓ   29. Ⓐ Ⓑ Ⓒ Ⓓ

10. Ⓐ Ⓑ Ⓒ Ⓓ   20. Ⓐ Ⓑ Ⓒ Ⓓ   30. Ⓐ Ⓑ Ⓒ Ⓓ

Mathematics Answer Sheet

1. (A) (B) (C) (D)   11. (A) (B) (C) (D)   21. (A) (B) (C) (D)

2. (A) (B) (C) (D)   12. (A) (B) (C) (D)   22. (A) (B) (C) (D)

3. (A) (B) (C) (D)   13. (A) (B) (C) (D)   23. (A) (B) (C) (D)

4. (A) (B) (C) (D)   14. (A) (B) (C) (D)   24. (A) (B) (C) (D)

5. (A) (B) (C) (D)   15. (A) (B) (C) (D)   25. (A) (B) (C) (D)

6. (A) (B) (C) (D)   16. (A) (B) (C) (D)   26. (A) (B) (C) (D)

7. (A) (B) (C) (D)   17. (A) (B) (C) (D)   27. (A) (B) (C) (D)

8. (A) (B) (C) (D)   18. (A) (B) (C) (D)   28. (A) (B) (C) (D)

9. (A) (B) (C) (D)   19. (A) (B) (C) (D)   29. (A) (B) (C) (D)

10. (A) (B) (C) (D)   20. (A) (B) (C) (D)   30. (A) (B) (C) (D)

Writing Skills Answer Sheet

1. Ⓐ Ⓑ Ⓒ Ⓓ   11. Ⓐ Ⓑ Ⓒ Ⓓ   21. Ⓐ Ⓑ Ⓒ Ⓓ

2. Ⓐ Ⓑ Ⓒ Ⓓ   12. Ⓐ Ⓑ Ⓒ Ⓓ   22. Ⓐ Ⓑ Ⓒ Ⓓ

3. Ⓐ Ⓑ Ⓒ Ⓓ   13. Ⓐ Ⓑ Ⓒ Ⓓ   23. Ⓐ Ⓑ Ⓒ Ⓓ

4. Ⓐ Ⓑ Ⓒ Ⓓ   14. Ⓐ Ⓑ Ⓒ Ⓓ   24. Ⓐ Ⓑ Ⓒ Ⓓ

5. Ⓐ Ⓑ Ⓒ Ⓓ   15. Ⓐ Ⓑ Ⓒ Ⓓ   25. Ⓐ Ⓑ Ⓒ Ⓓ

6. Ⓐ Ⓑ Ⓒ Ⓓ   16. Ⓐ Ⓑ Ⓒ Ⓓ   26. Ⓐ Ⓑ Ⓒ Ⓓ

7. Ⓐ Ⓑ Ⓒ Ⓓ   17. Ⓐ Ⓑ Ⓒ Ⓓ   27. Ⓐ Ⓑ Ⓒ Ⓓ

8. Ⓐ Ⓑ Ⓒ Ⓓ   18. Ⓐ Ⓑ Ⓒ Ⓓ   28. Ⓐ Ⓑ Ⓒ Ⓓ

9. Ⓐ Ⓑ Ⓒ Ⓓ   19. Ⓐ Ⓑ Ⓒ Ⓓ   29. Ⓐ Ⓑ Ⓒ Ⓓ

10. Ⓐ Ⓑ Ⓒ Ⓓ   20. Ⓐ Ⓑ Ⓒ Ⓓ   30. Ⓐ Ⓑ Ⓒ Ⓓ

Part 1 - Reading

Questions 1 - 4 refer to the following passage.

Infectious Diseases

An infectious disease is a clinically evident illness resulting from the presence of pathogenic agents, such as viruses, bacteria, fungi, protozoa, multi-cellular parasites, and unusual proteins known as prions. Infectious pathologies are also called communicable diseases or transmissible diseases, due to their potential of transmission from one person or species to another by a replicating agent (as opposed to a toxin).

Transmission of an infectious disease can occur in many different ways. Physical contact, liquids, food, body fluids, contaminated objects, and airborne inhalation can all transmit infecting agents.

Transmissible diseases that occur through contact with an ill person, or objects touched by them, are especially infective, and are sometimes called contagious diseases. Communicable diseases that require a more specialized route of infection, such as through blood or needle transmission, or sexual transmission, are usually not regarded as contagious.

The term infectivity describes the ability of an organism to enter, survive and multiply in the host, while the infectiousness of a disease indicates the comparative ease with which the disease is transmitted. An infection however, is not synonymous with an infectious disease, as an infection may not cause important clinical symptoms. [3]

1. What can we infer from the first paragraph in this passage?

a. Sickness from a toxin can be easily transmitted from one person to another.

b. Sickness from an infectious disease can be easily transmitted from one person to another.

c. Few sicknesses are transmitted from one person to another.

d. Infectious diseases are easily treated.

2. What are two other names for infections' pathologies?

a. Communicable diseases or transmissible diseases

b. Communicable diseases or terminal diseases

c. Transmissible diseases or preventable diseases

d. Communicative diseases or unstable diseases

3. What does infectivity describe?

a. The inability of an organism to multiply in the host.

b. The inability of an organism to reproduce.

c. The ability of an organism to enter, survive and multiply in the host.

d. The ability of an organism to reproduce in the host.

4. How do we know an infection is not synonymous with an infectious disease?

a. Because an infectious disease destroys infections with enough time.

b. Because an infection may not cause clinical symptoms or impair host function.

c. We do not. The two are synonymous.

d. Because an infection is too fatal to be an infectious disease.

Questions 5 – 7 refer to the following passage.

Thunderstorms

The first stage of a thunderstorm is the cumulus stage, or developing stage. In this stage, masses of moisture are lifted upwards into the atmosphere. The trigger for this lift can be insulation heating the ground producing thermals, areas where two winds converge, forcing air upwards, or, where winds blow over terrain of increasing elevation. Moisture in the air rapidly cools into liquid drops of water, which appears as cumulus clouds.

As the water vapor condenses into liquid, latent heat is released which warms the air, causing it to become less dense than the surrounding dry air. The warm air rises in an updraft through the process of convection (hence the term convective precipitation). This creates a low-pressure zone beneath the forming thunderstorm. In a typical thunderstorm, about 5×10^8 kg of water vapor is lifted, and the quantity of energy released when this condenses is about equal to the energy used by a city of 100,000 in a month. [4]

5. The cumulus stage of a thunderstorm is the

a. The last stage of the storm.

b. The middle stage of the storm formation.

c. The beginning of the thunderstorm.

d. The period after the thunderstorm has ended.

6. One way the air is warmed is

a. Air moving downwards, which creates a high-pressure zone.

b. Air cooling and becoming less dense, causing it to rise.

c. Moisture moving downward toward the earth.

d. Heat created by water vapor condensing into liquid.

7. Identify the correct sequence of events.

a. Warm air rises, water droplets condense, creating more heat, and the air rises farther.

b. Warm air rises and cools, water droplets condense, causing low pressure.

c. Warm air rises and collects water vapor, the water vapor condenses as the air rises, which creates heat, and causes the air to rise farther.

d. None of the above.

Questions 8 – 10 refer to the following passage.

The US Weather Service

The United States National Weather Service classifies thunderstorms as severe when they reach a predetermined level. Usually, this means the storm is strong enough to inflict wind or hail damage. In most of the United States, a storm is considered severe if winds reach over 50 knots (58 mph or 93 km/h), hail is ¾ inch (2 cm) diameter or larger, or if meteorologists report funnel clouds or tornadoes. In the Central Region of the United States National Weather Service, the hail threshold for a severe thunderstorm is 1 inch (2.5 cm) in diameter. Though a funnel cloud or tornado indicates the presence of a severe thunderstorm, the various meteorological agencies would issue a tornado warning rather than a severe thunderstorm warning here.

Meteorologists in Canada define a severe thunderstorm as either having tornadoes, wind gusts of 90 km/h or greater, hail 2 centimeters in diameter or greater, rainfall more than 50 millimeters in 1 hour, or 75 millimeters in 3 hours.

Severe thunderstorms can develop from any type of thunderstorm. [5]

8. What is the purpose of this passage?

a. Explaining when a thunderstorm turns into a tornado.

b. Explaining who issues storm warnings, and when these warnings should be issued.

c. Explaining when meteorologists consider a thunderstorm severe.

d. None of the above.

9. It is possible to infer from this passage that

a. Different areas and countries have different criteria for determining a severe storm.

b. Thunderstorms can include lightning and tornadoes, as well as violent winds and large hail.

c. If someone spots both a thunderstorm and a tornado, meteorological agencies will immediately issue a severe storm warning.

d. Canada has a much different alert system for severe storms, with criteria that are far less.

10. What would the Central Region of the United States National Weather Service do if hail was 2.7 cm in diameter?

a. Not issue a severe thunderstorm warning.

b. Issue a tornado warning.

c. Issue a severe thunderstorm warning.

d. Sleet must also accompany the hail before the Weather Service will issue a storm warning.

Questions 11 – 13 refer to the following passage.

Clouds

A cloud is a visible mass of droplets or frozen crystals float-ing in the atmosphere above the surface of the Earth or other planetary bodies. Another type of cloud is a mass of material in space, attracted by gravity, called interstellar clouds and nebulae. The branch of meteorology which stud-ies clouds is called nephrology. When we are speaking of Earth clouds, water vapor is usually the condensing sub-stance, which forms small droplets or ice crystal. These crys-tals are typically 0.01 mm in diameter. Dense, deep clouds reflect most light, so they appear white, at least from the top. Cloud droplets scatter light very efficiently, so the farther into a cloud light travels, the weaker it gets. This accounts for the gray or dark appearance at the base of large clouds. Thin clouds may appear to have acquired the color of their environment or background. [6]

11. What are clouds made of?

     a. Water droplets

     b. Ice crystals

     c. Ice crystals and water droplets

     d. Clouds on Earth are made of ice crystals and water droplets

12. The main idea of this passage is

     a. Condensation occurs in clouds, having an intense effect on the weather on the surface of the earth.

     b. Atmospheric gases are responsible for the gray color of clouds just before a severe storm happens.

     c. A cloud is a visible mass of droplets or frozen crys-tals floating in the atmosphere above the surface of the Earth or other planetary body.

     d. Clouds reflect light in varying amounts and degrees, depending on the size and concentration of the water droplets.

13. Why are clouds white on top and grey on the bottom?

a. Because water droplets inside the cloud do not reflect light, it appears white, and the farther into the cloud the light travels, the less light is reflected making the bottom appear dark.

b. Because water droplets outside the cloud reflect light, it appears dark, and the farther into the cloud the light travels, the more light is reflected making the bottom appear white.

c. Because water droplets inside the cloud reflects light, making it appear white, and the farther into the cloud the light travels, the more light is reflected making the bottom appear dark.

d. None of the above.

Questions 14 - 17 refer to the following passage.

Keeping Tropical Fish

Keeping tropical fish at home or in your office used to be very popular. Today, interest has declined, but it remains as rewarding and relaxing a hobby as ever. Ask any tropical fish hobbyist, and you will hear how soothing and relaxing watching colorful fish live their lives in the aquarium. If you are considering keeping tropical fish as pets, here is a list of the basic equipment you will need.

A filter is essential for keeping your aquarium clean and your fish alive and healthy. There are different types and sizes of filters and the right size for you depends on the size of the aquarium and the level of stocking. Generally, you need a filter with a 3 to 5 times turn over rate per hour. This means that the water in the tank should go through the filter about 3 to 5 times per hour.

Most tropical fish do well in water temperatures ranging between 24^{0}C and 26^{0}C, though each has its own ideal water temperature. A heater with a thermostat is necessary to regulate the water temperature. Some heaters are submersible and others are not, so check carefully before you buy.

Lights are also necessary, and come in a large variety of types, strengths and sizes. A light source is necessary for plants in the tank to photosynthesize and give the tank a more attractive appearance. Even if you plan to use plastic plants, the fish still require light, although here you can use a lower strength light source.

A hood is necessary to keep dust, dirt and unwanted materials out of the tank. Sometimes the hood can also help prevent evaporation. Another requirement is aquarium gravel. This will improve the aesthetics of the aquarium and is necessary if you plan to have real plants.

14. What is the general tone of this article?

a. Formal

b. Informal

c. Technical

d. Opinion

15. Which of the following can not be inferred?

a. Gravel is good for aquarium plants.

b. Fewer people have aquariums in their office than at home.

c. The larger the tank, the larger the filter required.

d. None of the above.

16. What evidence does the author provide to support their claim that aquarium lights are necessary?

a. Plants require light.

b. Fish and plants require light.

c. The author does not provide evidence for this statement.

d. Aquarium lights make the aquarium more attractive.

17. Which of the following is an opinion?

a. Filter with a 3 to 5 times turn over rate per hour are required.

b. Aquarium gravel improves the aesthetics of the aquarium.

c. An aquarium hood keeps dust, dirt and unwanted materials out of the tank.

d. Each type of tropical fish has its own ideal water temperature.

Questions 18 - 20 refer to the following passage.

Ways Characters Communicate in Theater

Playwrights give their characters voices in a way that gives depth and added meaning to what happens on stage during their play. There are different types of speech in scripts that allow characters to talk with themselves, with other characters, and even with the audience.

It is very unique to theater that characters may talk "to themselves." When characters do this, the speech they give is called a soliloquy. Soliloquies are usually poetic, introspective, moving, and can tell audience members about the feelings, motivations, or suspicions of an individual character without that character having to reveal them to other characters on stage. "To be or not to be" is a famous soliloquy given by Hamlet as he considers difficult but important themes, such as life and death.

The most common type of communication in plays is when one character is speaking to another or a group of other characters. This is generally called dialogue, but can also be called monologue if one character speaks without being interrupted for a long time. It is not necessarily the most important type of communication, but it is the most common because the plot of the play cannot really progress without it.
Lastly, and most unique to theater (although it has been

used somewhat in film) is when a character speaks directly to the audience. This is called an aside, and scripts usually specifically direct actors to do this. Asides are usually comical, an inside joke between the character and the audience, and very short. The actor will usually face the audience when delivering them, even if it's for a moment, so the audience can recognize this move as an aside.

All three of these types of communication are important to the art of theater, and have been perfected by famous playwrights like Shakespeare. Understanding these types of communication can help an audience member grasp what is artful about the script and action of a play. [7]

18. According to the passage, characters in plays communicate to

    a. move the plot forward

    b. show the private thoughts and feelings of one character

    c. make the audience laugh

    d. add beauty and artistry to the play

19. When Hamlet delivers "To be or not to be," he can most likely be described as

    a. solitary

    b. thoughtful

    c. dramatic

    d. hopeless

20. The author uses parentheses to punctuate "although it has been used somewhat in film"

a. to show that films are less important

b. instead of using commas so that the sentence is not interrupted

c. because parenthesis help separate details that are not as important

d. to show that films are not as artistic

Questions 21 - 24 refer to the following passage.

Frankenstein

Great God! What a scene has just taken place! I am yet dizzy with the remembrance of it. I hardly know whether I shall have the power to detail it; yet the tale which I have recorded would be incomplete without this final and wonderful catastrophe. I entered the cabin where lay the remains of my ill-fated and admirable friend. Over him hung a form which I cannot find words to describe—gigantic in stature, yet uncouth and distorted in its proportions. As he hung over the coffin, his face was concealed by long locks of ragged hair; but one vast hand was extended, in color and apparent texture like that of a mummy. When he heard the sound of my approach, he ceased to utter exclamations of grief and horror and sprung towards the window. Never did I behold a vision so horrible as his face, of such loathsome yet appalling hideousness. I shut my eyes involuntarily and endeavored to recollect what were my duties with regard to this destroyer. I called on him to stay.

He paused, looking on me with wonder, and again turning towards the lifeless form of his creator, he seemed to forget my presence, and every feature and gesture seemed instigated by the wildest rage of some uncontrollable passion.

"That is also my victim!" he exclaimed. "In his murder my crimes are consummated; the miserable series of my being is wound to its close! Oh, Frankenstein! Generous and self-devoted being! What does it avail that I now ask thee to pardon me? I, who irretrievably destroyed thee by destroying all thou lovedst. Alas! He is cold, he cannot answer me."

His voice seemed suffocated, and my first impulses, which had suggested to me the duty of obeying the dying request of my friend in destroying his enemy, were now suspended by a mixture of curiosity and compassion. I approached this tremendous being; I dared not again raise my eyes to his face, there was something so scaring and unearthly in his ugliness. I attempted to speak, but the words died away on my lips. The monster continued to utter wild and incoherent self-reproaches. At length I gathered resolution to address him in a pause of the tempest of his passion.

"Your repentance," I said, "is now superfluous. If you had listened to the voice of conscience and heeded the stings of remorse before you had urged your diabolical vengeance to this extremity, Frankenstein would yet have lived." [7]

21. Who is the "ill-fated and admirable friend" who is lying in the coffin?

   a. Frankenstein's monster

   b. Frankenstein

   c. Mary Shelley

   d. Unknown

22. Why is the speaker 'suspended" from following through on his duty to destroy the monster?

   a. The way the monster looks

   b. The monster's remorse

   c. Curiosity and compassion

   d. Fear the monster might kill him too

23. How does Frankenstein's monster destroy Frankenstein?

a. By killing Frankenstein

b. By letting himself be the monster everyone sees him as

c. By destroying everything Frankenstein loved

d. All of the above

24. When the Speaker says the monster's repentance is "superfluous, what does he mean?

a. That it is unnecessary and unused because Frankenstein is already dead and cannot hear him

b. That he accepts the repentance on behalf of Frankenstein

c. That the monster does not actually feel remorseful

d. That his repentance is unneeded because he did not do anything wrong

Questions 24 - 26 refer to the following passage.

Scotland's Windy Power Source

The Scottish Government has a targeted plan of generating 100% of Scotland's electricity through renewable energy by 2020. Renewable energy sources include sun, water and wind power. Scotland uses all forms but its fastest growing energy is wind energy. Wind power is generated through the use of wind turbines, placed onshore and offshore. Wind turbines that are grouped together in large numbers are called wind farms. Most Scottish citizens say that the wind farms are necessary to meet current and future energy needs, and would like to see an increase in the number of wind farms. They cite the fact that wind energy does not cause pollution, there are low operational costs, and most importantly due to the definition of renewable energy it cannot be depleted.

25. What is Scotland's fastest growing source of renewable energy?

a. Solar Panels

b. Hydroelectric

c. Wind

d. Fossil Fuels

26. Why do most Scottish citizens agree with the Government's plan?

a. Their concern for current and future energy needs

b. Because of the low operational costs

c. Because they are out of sight

d. Because it provides jobs

Questions 27 - 28 refer to the following passage.

Scotland's Windy Power Source II

However, there is still a public debate concerning the use of wind farms to generate energy. The most cited argument against wind energy is that the up front investment is expensive. They also argue that it is aesthetically displeasing, they are noisy, and they create a serious threat to wildlife in the area. While wind energy is renewable, or cannot be depleted, it does not mean that wind is always available. Wind is fluctuating, or intermittent, and therefore not suited to meet the base amount of energy demand, meaning if there is no wind then no energy is being created.

27. What is the biggest argument against wind energy?

a. The turbines are noisy

b. The turbines endanger wildlife

c. The turbines are expensive to build

d. They are aesthetically displeasing

28. What is the best way to describe this article's description of wind energy?

a. Loud and ever present

b. The cheapest form of renewable energy

c. The only source of renewable energy in Scotland

d. Clean and renewable but fluctuating

Questions 29 - 30 refer to the following passage.

The Civil War

The Civil War began on April 12, 1861. The first shots of the Civil War were fired in Fort Sumter, South Carolina. Note that even though more American lives were lost in the Civil War than in any other war, not one person died on that first day. The war began because eleven Southern states seceded from the Union and tried to start their own government, The Confederate States of America.

Why did the states secede? The issue of slavery was a primary cause of the Civil War. The eleven southern states relied heavily on their slaves to foster their farming and plantation lifestyles. The northern states, many of whom had already abolished slavery, did not feel that the southern states should have slaves. The north wanted to free all the slaves and President Lincoln's goal was to both end slavery and preserve the Union. He had Congress declare war on the Confederacy on April 14, 1862. For four long, blood soaked years, the North and South fought.

From 1861 to mid 1863, it seemed as if the South would win this war. However, on July 1, 1863, an epic three day battle was waged on a field in Gettysburg, Pennsylvania. Gettysburg is remembered for being the bloodiest battle in American history. At the end of the three days, the North turned the tide of the war in their favor. The North then went onto dominate the South for the remainder of the war. Most well remembered might be General Sherman's "March to The Sea," where he famously led the Union Army through Georgia and the Carolinas, burning and destroying everything in their path.

In 1865, the Union army invaded and captured the Confederate capital of Richmond Virginia. Robert E. Lee, leader of the Confederacy surrendered to General Ulysses S. Grant, leader of the Union forces, on April 9, 1865. The Civil War was over, and the Union was preserved.

29. What does the word secede most nearly mean?

     a. To break away from

     b. To accomplish

     c. To join

     d. To lose

30. Which of the following statements summarizes a FACT from the passage?

     a. Congress declared war and then the Battle of Fort Sumter began.

     b. Congress declared war after shots were fired at Fort Sumter.

     c. President Lincoln was pro slavery

     d. President Lincoln was at Fort Sumter with Congress

Mathematics

1. Divide 243 by 3^3

    a. 243

    b. 11

    c. 9

    d. 27

2. Solve the following equation $4(y + 6) = 3y + 30$

    a. $y = 20$

    b. $y = 6$

    c. $y = 30/7$

    d. $y = 30$

3. Divide $x^2 - y^2$ by $x - y$.

    a. $x - y$

    b. $x + y$

    c. xy

    d. $y - x$

4. Solve for x if, $10^2 \times 100^2 = 1000^x$

    a. $x = 2$

    b. $x = 3$

    c. $x = -2$

    d. $x = 0$

5. Given polynomials A = -2x⁴ + x² - 3x, B = x⁴ - x³ + 5 and C = x⁴ + 2x³ + 4x + 5, find A + B - C.

  a. $x^3 + x^2 + x + 10$

  b. $-3x^3 + x^2 - 7x + 10$

  c. $-2x^4 - 3x^3 + x^2 - 7x$

  d. $-3x^4 + x^3 + 2 - 7x$

6. Solve the inequality: $(x - 6)^2 \geq x^2 + 12$

  a. $(2, + \infty)$

  b. $(2, + \infty)$

  c. $(-\infty, 2)$

  d. $(12, + \infty)$

7. $7^5 - 3^5 =$

  a. 15,000

  b. 16,564

  c. 15,800

  d. 15,007

8. Divide $x^3 - 3x^2 + 3x - 1$ by $x - 1$.

  a. $x^2 - 1$

  b. $x^2 + 1$

  c. $x^2 - 2x + 1$

  d. $x^2 + 2x + 1$

9. Express 9 x 9 x 9 in exponential form and standard form.

  a. $9^3 = 719$

  b. $9^3 = 629$

  c. $9^3 = 729$

  d. $10^3 = 729$

10. Using the factoring method, solve the quadratic equation: $x^2 - 5x - 6 = 0$

  a. -6 and 1

  b. -1 and 6

  c. 1 and 6

  d. -6 and -1

11. Divide 0.524 by 10^3

  a. 0.0524

  b. 0.00052

  c. 0.00524

  d. 524

12. Factor the polynomial $x^3y^3 - x^2y^8$.

  a. $x^2y^3(x - y^5)$

  b. $x^3y^3(1 - y^5)$

  c. $x^2y^2(x - y^6)$

  d. $xy^3(x - y^5)$

13. Find the solution for the following linear equation: $5x/2 = 3x + 24/6$

  a. -1

  b. 0

  c. 1

  d. 2

14. $3^2 \times 3^5$

  a. 3^{17}

  b. 3^5

  c. 4^8

  d. 3^7

15. Solve the system, if a is some real number:

ax + y = 1
x + ay = 1

    a. (1,a)

    b. (1/a + 1, 1)

    c. (1/a = 1, 1/a + 1)

    d. (a, 1/a + 1)

16. Solve $3^5 \div 3^8$

    a. 3^3

    b. 3^5

    c. 3^6

    d. 3^4

17. Solve the linear equation: 3(x + 2) - 2(1 - x) = 4x + 5

    a. -1

    b. 0

    c. 1

    d. 2

18. Simplify the following expression: $3x^a + 6a^x - x^a + (-5a^x) - 2x^a$

    a. $a^x + x^a$

    b. $a^x - x^a$

    c. a^x

    d. x^a

19. Add polynomials -3x² + 2x + 6 and -x² - x - 1.

  a. -2x² + x + 5

  b. -4x² + x + 5

  c. -2x² + 3x + 5

  d. -4x² + 3x + 5

20. 10⁴ is not equal to which of the following?

  a. 100,000

  b. 10 x 10 x 10 x 10

  c. 10² x 10²

  d. 10,000

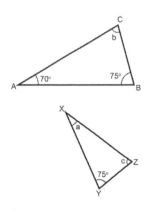

21. What are the respective values of a, b & c if both triangles are similar?

  a. 70°, 70°, 35°

  b. 70°, 35°, 70°

  c. 35°, 35°, 35°

  d. 70°, 35°, 35°

22. Consider 2 triangles, ABC and A'B'C', where:

BC = B' C'

AC = A' C'

RA = RA'

Are these 2 triangles congruent?

a. Yes

b. No

c. Not enough information

23. What is the perimeter of ΔABC in the above shape?

a. 25.5 cm

b. 27 cm

c. 30 cm

d. 29 cm

24. If angle α is equal to the expression 3π/2 - π/6 - π - π/3, find sinα.

a. 0

b. 1/2

c. 1

d. 3/2

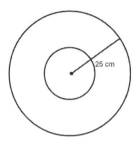

25 cm

25. What is the distance travelled by the wheel above, when it makes 175 revolutions?

    a. 87.5 π m

    b. 875 π m

    c. 8.75 π m

    d. 8750 π m

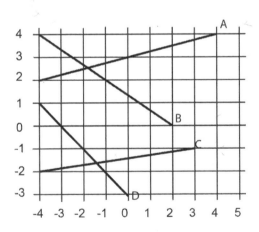

26. Which of the lines above represents the equation 2y − x = 4?

a. A

b. B

c. C

d. D

27. Find the sides of a right triangle whose sides are consecutive numbers.

    a. 1, 2, 3

    b. 2, 3, 4

    c. 3, 4, 5

    d. 4, 5, 6

28. What is the length of the sides in the triangle above?

    a. 10

    b. 20

    c. 100

    d. 40

29. Calculate the length of side x.

    a. 6.46

    b. 8.46

    c. 3.6

    d. 6.4

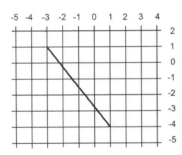

30. What is the slope of the line shown above?

    a. 5/4

    b. -4/5

    c. -5/4

    d. -4/5

Writing

Directions: For questions 1 - 3, read the short passage answer the question.

Alvin Lee began playing guitar at an early age, and was influenced by his parents' passion for music and inspired by the likes of Chuck Berry and Scotty Moore. [1] Lee started his career as the lead vocalist and guitarist in a band named the Jaybirds at the famous Marquee Club in London in 1962. [2] A few years later the band changed its name to Ten Years After, and released its debut album under the new name. [3] Lee's lightning fast guitar playing at the Woodstock Festival gained him instant stardom and Lee was asked to tour the US. [4]

1. Which sentence in the second paragraph is the least relevant to the main idea of the second paragraph?

    a. 1

    b. 2

    c. 3

    d. 4

Curiosity was launched in late November 2011 from Cape Canaveral Air Force Station in Florida. [1] It successfully landed on Mars on August 6, 2012 searching for evidence of life. [2] The car sized robot, weighing about a ton, is equipped with all the technical capacities to carry out its mission to explore our neighbor for biological, geological and geochemical traces of life. [3] It will also test the Martian soil and surface to collect data about its planetary evolution and surface radiation. [4]

2. Which sentence is the least relevant to the main idea of the third paragraph?

    a. 1

    b. 2

    c. 3

    d. 4

With an estimated 100,000 species, trees represent 25 percent of all living plant species. Most tree species grow in tropical regions of the world and many of these areas have not been surveyed by botanists, making species diversity poorly understood. The earliest trees were tree ferns and horsetails, which grew in forests in the Carboniferous period. Tree ferns still survive, but the only surviving horsetails are no longer in tree form. Later, in the Triassic period, conifers and ginkgos, appeared, followed by flowering plants after that in the Cretaceous period. [5]

3. Choose the correct list below, ranked from oldest to youngest trees.

    a. Flowering plants, conifers and ginkgos, tree ferns and horsetails

    b. Tree ferns and horsetails, conifers and ginkgos, flowering plants

    c. Tree ferns and horsetails, flowering plants, conifers and ginkgos

    d. Conifers and ginkgos, tree ferns and horsetails, flowering plants

Directions: Choose the word or phrase that best completes the sentence.

4. The Ford Motor Company was named for Henry Ford, _____ had founded the company.

  a. which

  b. who

  c. whose

  d. None of the options are correct.

5. Thomas Edison _____ as the greatest inventor since he invented the light bulb, television, motion pictures, and phonograph.

  a. has always been known

  b. was always been known

  c. must have had been always known

  d. None of the options are correct.

6. The weatherman on Channel 6 said that this has been the _____ summer on record.

  a. most hottest

  b. hottest

  c. hotter

  d. None of the options are correct.

7. Although Joe is tall for his age, his brother Elliot is _____ of the two.

  a. tallest

  b. tall of the two.

  c. the taller

  d. None of the options are correct.

8. When KISS came to town, all the tickets _____ sold out before I could buy one.

    a. will be

    b. had been

    c. were being

    d. None of the options are correct.

9. The rules of most sports _____ more complicated than we often realize.

    a. are

    b. is

    c. was

    d. None of the options are correct.

10. Neither of the Wright Brothers _____ any doubts that they would be successful with their flying machine.

    a. have

    b. has

    c. had

    d. None of the options are correct.

11. The Titanic _____ mere days into its maiden voyage.

    a. will already sunk

    b. sank

    c. had sank

    d. None of the choices are correct.

12. When he's _____ friends, Robert seems confident.

    a. None of the choices are correct.

    b. between

    c. among

13. His home was _____ than we expected.

    a. The sentence is correct.

    b. farther

    c. None of the choices are correct.

14. The tables were _____ by the students.

    a. laid

    b. lay

    c. lie

    d. None of the choices are correct.

15. Each boy and girl _____ given a toy.

    a. were

    b. was

    c. Either A or B can be used.

    d. None of the choices are correct.

16. His measles _____ getting better.

    a. is

    b. are

    c. Either A or B can be used.

    d. None of the choices are correct.

17. Despite the bad weather yesterday, he ____ still attend the party.

    a. The sentence is correct.

    b. could

    c. may

    d. None of the choices are correct.

18. Choose the sentence with the correct punctuation.

    a. To make chicken soup you must first buy a chicken.

    b. To make chicken soup you must first, buy a chicken.

    c. To make chicken soup, you must first buy a chicken.

    d. None of the choices are correct.

19. Choose the sentence with the correct punctuation.

    a. To travel around the globe, you have to drive 25000 miles.

    b. To travel around the globe, you have to drive, 25000 miles.

    c. None of the choices are correct.

    d. To travel around the globe, you have to drive 25,000 miles.

20. Choose the sentence with the correct punctuation.

    a. The dog loved chasing bones, but never ate them; it was running that he enjoyed.

    b. The dog loved chasing bones; but never ate them, it was running that he enjoyed.

    c. The dog loved chasing bones, but never ate them, it was running that he enjoyed.

    d. None of the choices are correct.

21. Choose the sentence with the correct punctuation.

a. However, I believe that he didn't really try that hard.
b. However I believe that he didn't really try that hard.
c. None of the choices are correct.
d. However: I believe that he didn't really try that hard.

22. Choose the sentence that is written correctly.

a. Any girl that fails the test loses their admission.
b. Any girl that fails the test loses our admission.
c. Any girl that fails the test loses <u>her</u> admission.
d. None of the choices are correct.

23. Choose the sentence that is written correctly.

a. He ought to be back by now.
b. He ought be back by now.
c. He ought come back by now.
d. None of the choices are correct.

24. Choose the sentence that is written correctly.

a. The man as well as his son has arrived
b. The man as well as his son have arrived.
c. None of the choices are correct.

25. Choose the sentence that is written correctly.

a. Mark and Peter have talked to each other.
b. Mark and Peter have talked to one another.
c. None of the choices are correct.

26. Choose the sentence that is written correctly.

a. Christians believe that their lord have raised.

b. Christians believe that their lord has risen.

c. Christians believe that their lord have raise.

d. None of the choices are correct.

27. Choose the sentence that is written correctly.

a. Here are the names of people whom you should contact.

b. Here are the names of people who you should contact

c. None of the choices are correct.

28. Choose the sentence that is written correctly.

a. The World Health Organization (WHO) are meeting by January.

b. The World Health Organization (WHO) is meeting by January.

c. None of the choices are correct.

29. Choose the sentence that is written correctly.

a. They will have to retire when they reach 60 years of age.

b. They shall have to retire when they reach 60 years of age.

c. None of the choices are correct.

Directions: Choose the sentence that best support the topic sentence below.

30. Volcanoes occur because the planet's crust is broken into 17 major tectonic plates that float on a hotter, softer layer in the Earth's mantle.

a. Therefore, volcanoes are generally found where tectonic plates are diverging or converging.

b. Volcanoes generally cause extensive damage to property.

c. Volcanoes do not often erupt, but can be spectacular when they do.

c. Most volcanoes are far from major urban centers.

Answer Key

Reading

1. B
We can infer from this passage that sickness from an infectious disease can be easily transmitted from one person to another.

From the passage, "Infectious pathologies are also called communicable diseases or transmissible diseases, due to their potential of transmission from one person or species to another by a replicating agent (as opposed to a toxin)."

2. A
Two other names for infectious pathologies are communicable diseases and transmissible diseases.

From the passage, "Infectious pathologies are also called communicable diseases or transmissible diseases, due to their potential of transmission from one person or species to another by a replicating agent (as opposed to a toxin)."

3. C
Infectivity describes the ability of an organism to enter, survive and multiply in the host. This is taken directly from the passage, and is a definition type question.

Definition type questions can be answered quickly and easily by scanning the passage for the word you are asked to define.

"Infectivity" is an unusual word, so it is quick and easy to scan the passage looking for this word.

4. B
We know an infection is not synonymous with an infectious disease because an infection may not cause important clinical symptoms or impair host function.

5. C
The cumulus stage of a thunderstorm is the beginning of the

thunderstorm.

This is taken directly from the passage, "The first stage of a thunderstorm is the cumulus, or developing stage."

6. D
The passage lists four ways that air is heated. One way is, heat created by water vapor condensing into liquid.

7. A
The sequence of events can be taken from these sentences:

As the moisture carried by the [1] air currents rises, it rapidly cools into liquid drops of water, which appear as cumulus clouds. As the water vapor condenses into liquid, it [2] releases heat, which warms the air. This in turn causes the air to become less dense than the surrounding dry air and [3] rise farther.

8. C
The purpose of this text is to explain when meteorologists consider a thunderstorm severe.

The main idea is the first sentence, "The United States National Weather Service classifies thunderstorms as severe when they reach a predetermined level." After the first sentence, the passage explains and elaborates on this idea. Everything is this passage is related to this idea, and there are no other major ideas in this passage that are central to the whole passage.

9. A
From this passage, we can infer that different areas and countries have different criteria for determining a severe storm.

From the passage we can see that most of the US has a criteria of, winds over 50 knots (58 mph or 93 km/h), and hail ¾ inch (2 cm). For the Central US, hail must be 1 inch (2.5 cm) in diameter. In Canada, winds must be 90 km/h or greater, hail 2 centimeters in diameter or greater, and rainfall more than 50 millimeters in 1 hour, or 75 millimeters in 3 hours.

Choice D is incorrect because the Canadian system is the same for hail, 2 centimeters in diameter.

10. C
With hail above the minimum size of 2.5 cm. diameter, the Central Region of the United States National Weather Service would issue a severe thunderstorm warning.

11. D
Clouds in space are made of different materials attracted by gravity. Clouds on Earth are made of water droplets or ice crystals.

Choice D is the best answer. Notice also that Choice D is the most specific.

12. C
The main idea is the first sentence of the passage; a cloud is a visible mass of droplets or frozen crystals floating in the atmosphere above the surface of the Earth or other planetary body.

The main idea is very often the first sentence of the paragraph.

13. C
This question asks about the process, and gives choices that can be confirmed or eliminated easily.

From the passage, "Dense, deep clouds reflect most light, so they appear white, at least from the top. Cloud droplets scatter light very efficiently, so the farther into a cloud light travels, the weaker it gets. This accounts for the gray or dark appearance at the base of large clouds."

We can eliminate choice A, since water droplets inside the cloud do not reflect light is false.

We can eliminate choice B, since, water droplets outside the cloud reflect light, it appears dark, is false.

Choice C is correct.

14. B
The general tone is informal.

15. B
The statement, " Fewer people have aquariums in their office than at home," cannot be inferred from this article.

16. C
The author does not provide evidence for this statement.

17. B
The following statement is an opinion, " Aquarium gravel improves the aesthetics of the aquarium."

18. D
This question tests the reader's summarization skills. The question is asking very generally about the message of the passage, and the title, "Ways Characters Communicate in Theater," is one indication of that. The other choices, A, B, and C are all directly from the text, and therefore readers may be inclined to select one of them, but are too specific to encapsulate the entirety of the passage and its message.

19. B
The paragraph on soliloquies mentions "To be or not to be," and it is from the context of that paragraph that readers may understand that because "To be or not to be" is a soliloquy, Hamlet will be introspective, or thoughtful, while delivering it. It is true that actors deliver soliloquies alone, and may be "solitary" (choice A), but "thoughtful" (choice B) is more true to the overall idea of the paragraph. Readers may choose C because drama and theater can be used interchangeably and the passage mentions that soliloquies are unique to theater (and therefore drama), but this answer is not specific enough to the paragraph in question. Readers may pick up on the theme of life and death and Hamlet's true intentions and select that he is "hopeless" (choice D), but those themes are not discussed either by this paragraph or passage, as a close textual reading and analysis confirms.

20. C
This question tests the reader's grammatical skills. Choice B seems logical, but parenthesis are actually considered to be a stronger break in a sentence than commas are, and along this line of thinking, actually disrupt the sentence more.

Choices A and D make comparisons between theater and film that are simply not made in the passage, and may or may not be true. This detail does clarify the statement that asides are most unique to theater by adding that it is not completely unique to theater, which may have been why the author didn't chose not to delete it and instead used parentheses to designate the detail's importance (choice C).

21. B
Choice A is incorrect as the Monster killed Frankenstein, not the other way around. Choice B is correct, Frankenstein is dead. Choice C is incorrect - Mary Shelley is the author. Choice D is incorrect, the person is called Frankenstein.

22. C
the speaker 'suspended" from following through on his duty to destroy the monster due to curiosity and compassion. The other choices may seem reasonable, but are not explicitly given in the passage.

23. D
All of the choices are correct. Frankenstein's monster destroys Frankenstein by

    a. By killing Frankenstein

    b. By letting himself be the monster everyone sees him as

    c. By destroying everything Frankenstein loved

24. A
Superfluous means unnecessary. Looking at the context of the word as it is used in the passage:

"Your repentance," I said, "is now superfluous. If you had listened to the voice of conscience and heeded the stings of

remorse before you had urged your diabolical vengeance to
this extremity, Frankenstein would yet have lived."
25. C
Wind is the highest source of renewable energy in Scotland.
The other choices are either not mentioned at all or not mentioned in the context for how fast they are growing.

26. A
Most Scottish citizens agree with the Government's plan due
to the concern for current and future needs. Choice B is
a good choice but not why the majority agree. Choice C is
meant to mislead the as they are clearly in sight. Choice D
is a good 'common sense' choice but mentioned specifically
in the text.

27. C
The up-front cost is expensive.
The other choices may appear to be correct, and even be
common sense, but they are not specifically mentioned in
the paragraph.

28. D
The best way to describe the paragraphs description of wind
energy is clean and renewable but fluctuating.
The other choices are good descriptions of wind energy, but
not the best way to describe the article.

29. A
Secede means to break away from because the 11 states
wanted to leave the United States and form their own country. Choice B is incorrect because the states were not accomplishing anything Choice C is incorrect because the states
were trying to leave the USA not join it. Choice D is incorrect because the states seceded before they lost the war.

30. B
Look at the dates in the passage. The shots were fired on
April 12 and Congress declared war on April 14. Choice A
is incorrect because the dates show clearly which happened
first. Choice C is incorrect because the passage states that
Lincoln was against slavery. Choice D is incorrect because it
never mentions who was or was not at Fort Sumter.

Mathematics

1. C
243/3 x 3 x 3 = 243/27 = 9

2. B
4y + 24 = 3y + 30, = 4y – 3y + 24 = 30, = y + 24 = 30, = y =
30 – 24, = y = 6

3. B
$(x^2 - y^2) / (x - y) = x + y$

$\underline{-(x^2 - xy)}$
   $xy - y^2$

$\underline{-(xy - y^2)}$
      0

4. A
10 x 10 x 100 x 100 = 1000^x, =100 x 10,000 = 1000^x, =
1,000,000 = 1000^x = x = 2

5. C
A + B - C = $(-2x^4 + x^2 - 3x) + (x^4 - x^3 + 5) - (x^4 + 2x^3 + 4x + 5)$
$-2x^4 + x^2 - 3x + x^4 - x^3 + 5 - x^4 - 2x^3 - 4x - 5$
$-2x^4 - 3x^3 + x^2 - 7x$

6. C
$(x - 6)^2 \geq x^2 + 12$
$x^2 - 12x + 36 \geq x^2 + 12$
$-12x \geq 12 - 36$
$-12x \geq -24$
$-x \geq -2/-1$
$x \leq 2$

7. B
(7 x 7 x 7 x 7 x 7) - (3 x 3 x 3 x 3 x 3) = 16,807 – 243 =
16,564.

8. C
$(x^3 - 3x^2 + 3x - 1) / (x - 1) = x^2 - 2x + 1$
$\underline{-(x^3 - x^2)}$
      $-2x^2 + 3x - 1$

$$\frac{-(-2\ x^2 + 2x)}{x - 1}$$

$$\frac{-(x - 1)}{0}$$

9. C
Exponential form is 9^3 and standard from is 729

30. B
$x^2 - 5x - 6 = 0$
$x^2 - 6x + x - 6 = 0$
$x(x - 6) + x - 6 = 0$
$(x - 6)(x + 1) = 0$
$(x = 6)$ U $(x = -1)$

10. B
$x^2 - 5x - 6 = 0$
$x^2 - 6x + x - 6 = 0$
$x(x - 6) + x - 6 = 0$
$(x - 6)(x + 1) = 0$
$(x = 6)$ U $(x = -1)$

11. B
$0.524/\ 10 \times 10 \times 10 = 0.524/1000 = 0.000524$

12. A
$x^3y^3 - x^2y^8 = x *(x^2y^3 - x^2y^3 * y^5 = x^2y^3(x - y^5)$

13. D
$5x/2 = 3x + 24/6$
$3 * 5x/3 * 2 = 3x + 24/6$
$15x/6 = 3x + 24/6$
$15x = 3x + 24$
$15x - 3x = 25$
$12x = 24$
$x = 24/12 = 2$

14. D
When multiplying exponents with the same base, add the exponents. $3^2 \times 3^5 = 3^{2+5} = 3^7$

15. C
$y = 1 - ax$

x + a(1 - ax) = 1
x + a - a²x = 1
x(1 - a²) = 1 - a
x = 1 - a/1 = a² = 1 - a/(1 - a)(1 + a) = 1/a + 1

y = 1 - ax
y = 1 - a * 1/a + 1 = a/a + 1
y= a + 1 - a/a + 1 = 1/a + 1

16. A
To divide exponents with the same base, subtract the exponents. $3^{8-5} = 3^3$

17. C
3(x + 2) - 2(1 - x) = 4x + 5
3x + 6 - 2 + 2x = 4x + 5
5x + 4 = 4x + 5
5x - 4x = 5 - 4
x = 1

18. C
$3x^a + 6a^x - x^a + (-5a^x) - 2x^a = 3x^a + 6a^x - x^a - 5a^x - 2x^a = a^x$

19. B
$-4x^2 + x + 5$
$(-3x^2 + 2x + 6) + (-x^2 - x - 1)$
$-3x^2 + 2x + 6 - x^2 - x - 1$
$-4x^2 + x + 5$

20. A
10^4 is not equal to 100,000
$10^4 = 10 \times 10 \times 10 \times 10 = 10^2 \times 10^2 = 10,000$

21. D
Comparing angles on similar triangles, a, b and c will be 70°, 35°, 35°

22. A
Yes the triangles are congruent.

23. D
Perimeter of triangle ABC within two squares.
Perimeter = sum of the sides.

Perimeter = 8.5 + 8.5 + 6 + 6
Perimeter = 29 cm.

24. A

$a = 3\pi/2 - \pi/6 - \pi - \pi/3$
$(9\pi - \pi - 6\pi - 2\pi)/6$
$0\pi/6 = 0$
$\sin a = \sin 0^\circ = 0$

25. A

Diameter = 2 x radius.
Circumference = π x Diameter

Distance(meters) = (Circumference x Revolutions)/100
Distance(meters) = [((25 x 2) π) x 175]/100
Distance(meters) = 8750 π/100
Distance = 87.5 π meters.

26. A

Line A represents the equation $2y - x = 4$.

27. C

The length of the sides is, 3, 4, 5.
x
$y = x + 1$
$z = x + 2$
$x^2 + y^2 = y^2$
$x^2 + (x + 1)^2 = (x + 2)^2$
$x^2 + x^2 + 2x + 1 = x^2 + 4x + 4$
$x^2 - 2x - 3 \quad 0$

$x_{1,2} = 2 \pm \sqrt{4 + 12} \ / \ 2$
$x_{1,2} = 2 \pm 4 \ / \ 2$

$x = 3$
$y = 4$
$z = 5$

28. A

Pythagorean Theorem:

$(\text{Hypotenuse})^2 = (\text{Perpendicular})^2 + (\text{Base})^2$
$h^2 = a^2 + b^2$

Given: $h^2 = 200$, $a = b = x$
Then, $x^2 + x^2 = 200$, $2x^2 = 200$, $x^2 = 100$
$x = 10$

29. B
Pythagorean Theorem:
$(Hypotenuse)^2 = (Perpendicular)^2 + (Base)^2$
$h^2 = a^2 + b^2$

Given: d (diameter)= 12 & r (radius) = a = b = 6
$h^2 = a^2 + b^2$
$h^2 = 6^2 + 6^2$, $h^2 = 36 + 36$
$h^2 = 72$
$h = 8.46$

30. C
Slope (m) = change in y
 change in x

$(x_1, y_1)=(-3,1)$ & $(x_2, y_2)= (1,-4)$
Slope = $[-4 - 1]/[1-(-3)]= -5/4$

Writing

1. A
Sentence 1 is least relevant, "Alvin Lee began playing guitar at an early age, and was influenced by his parents' passion for music and inspired by the likes of Chuck Berry and Scotty Moore."

This sentence talks about Lee's motivation rather than his achievements, which is the main topic of the paragraph. Other sentences are related to a significant extent, but this sentence deviates from the main idea the most.

2. A
Sentence 1 is the least relevant. "Curiosity was launched in late November 2011 from Cape Canaveral Air Force Station in Florida."

This paragraph talks about the objectives of the rover.

All sentences other than sentence 2 mention the objectives. This sentence, however, informs us when the spacecraft was launched.

3. B
Here is the passage with the oldest to youngest trees

The earliest trees were [1] tree ferns and horsetails, which grew in forests in the Carboniferous period. Tree ferns still survive, but the only surviving horsetails are no longer in tree form. Later, in the Triassic period, [2] conifers and ginkgos, appeared, [3] followed by flowering plants after that in the Cretaceous period

4. B
The sentence refers to a person, so "who" is the only correct choice.

5. A
The sentence requires the past perfect "has always been known." The clue to this tense is the use of "since."

6. B
The superlative, "hottest," is used when expressing a temperature greater than that of anything to which it is being compared.

7. C
When comparing two items, use "the taller." When comparing more than two items, use "the tallest."

8. B
The past perfect form is used to describe an event that occurred in the past and before another event.

9. A
The subject is "rules" so the present tense plural form, "are," is used to agree with "realize."

10. C
The simple past tense, "had," is correct because it refers to completed action in the past.

11. B
The simple past tense, "sank," is correct because it refers to completed action in the past.

12. C
Among vs. Between. 'Among' is for more than 2 items, and 'between' is only for 2 items.

When he's among friends (many or more than 2), Robert seems confident, but, between you and me (two), he is very shy.

13. B
Further vs. Farther. 'Farther' is used for physical distance, and 'further' is used for figurative distance.

14. A
The verb "lay" should always take an object. Here the subject is the table. The three forms of the verb lay are: lay, laid and laid. The sentence above is in past tense.

15. B
Use the singular verb form when nouns are qualified with "every" or "each," even if they are joined by 'and. '

16. B
Use a plural verb for nouns like measles, tongs, trousers, riches, scissors etc.

17. B
Use "could," the past tense of "can" to express ability or capacity.

18. C
Comma separate phrases.

19. D
The comma separates clauses and numbers are separated with a comma. The correct sentence is,
'To travel around the globe, you have to drive 25,000 miles.'

20. A
The dog loved chasing bones, but never ate them; it was running that he enjoyed.

21. A
When using 'however,' place a comma before and after, except when however begins the sentence.

22. C
Words such as neither, each, many, either, every, everyone, everybody and any should take a singular pronoun.

23. A
The verb "ought" can be used to express desirability, duty and probability. The verb is usually followed by "to."

24. A
When two subjects are linked with "with" or "as well," use the verb form that matches the first subject.

25. A
When you use 'each other' it should be used for two things or people. When you use 'one another' it should be used for things and people above two

26. B
The verb rise ('to go up', 'to ascend.') can appear in three forms, rise, rose, and risen. The verb should not take an object.

27. A
The sentence is correct. Use "whom" in the objective case, and use "who" a subjective case.

28. B
Use a singular verb with a proper noun in plural form that refers to a single entity. Here, the The World Health Organization is a single entity, although it is made up on many members.

29. A
Will is used in the second or third person (they, he, she and you), while shall is used in the first person (I and we). Both verbs are used to express futurity.

30. A
Sentence A continues directly the discussion about tectonic plates. The other choices diverge from this central idea.

Practice Test Questions Set 2

The questions below are not the same as you will find on the PERT - that would be too easy! And nobody knows what the questions will be and they change all the time. Below are general questions that cover the same subject areas as the PERT. So, while the format and exact wording of the questions may differ slightly, and change from year to year, if you can answer the questions below, you will have no problem with the PERT.

For the best results, take these practice test questions as if it were the real exam. Set aside time when you will not be disturbed, and a location that is quiet and free of distractions. Read the instructions carefully, read each question carefully, and answer to the best of your ability.
Use the bubble answer sheets provided. When you have completed the Practice Questions, check your answer against the Answer Key and read the explanation provided.

Do not attempt more than one set of practice test questions in one day. After completing the first practice test, wait two or three days before attempting the second set of questions.

Reading Answer Sheet

1. (A) (B) (C) (D)　　11. (A) (B) (C) (D)　　21. (A) (B) (C) (D)

2. (A) (B) (C) (D)　　12. (A) (B) (C) (D)　　22. (A) (B) (C) (D)

3. (A) (B) (C) (D)　　13. (A) (B) (C) (D)　　23. (A) (B) (C) (D)

4. (A) (B) (C) (D)　　14. (A) (B) (C) (D)　　24. (A) (B) (C) (D)

5. (A) (B) (C) (D)　　15. (A) (B) (C) (D)　　25. (A) (B) (C) (D)

6. (A) (B) (C) (D)　　16. (A) (B) (C) (D)　　26. (A) (B) (C) (D)

7. (A) (B) (C) (D)　　17. (A) (B) (C) (D)　　27. (A) (B) (C) (D)

8. (A) (B) (C) (D)　　18. (A) (B) (C) (D)　　28. (A) (B) (C) (D)

9. (A) (B) (C) (D)　　19. (A) (B) (C) (D)　　29. (A) (B) (C) (D)

10. (A) (B) (C) (D)　　20. (A) (B) (C) (D)　　30. (A) (B) (C) (D)

Mathematics Answer Sheet

1. Ⓐ Ⓑ Ⓒ Ⓓ　11. Ⓐ Ⓑ Ⓒ Ⓓ　21. Ⓐ Ⓑ Ⓒ Ⓓ

2. Ⓐ Ⓑ Ⓒ Ⓓ　12. Ⓐ Ⓑ Ⓒ Ⓓ　22. Ⓐ Ⓑ Ⓒ Ⓓ

3. Ⓐ Ⓑ Ⓒ Ⓓ　13. Ⓐ Ⓑ Ⓒ Ⓓ　23. Ⓐ Ⓑ Ⓒ Ⓓ

4. Ⓐ Ⓑ Ⓒ Ⓓ　14. Ⓐ Ⓑ Ⓒ Ⓓ　24. Ⓐ Ⓑ Ⓒ Ⓓ

5. Ⓐ Ⓑ Ⓒ Ⓓ　15. Ⓐ Ⓑ Ⓒ Ⓓ　25. Ⓐ Ⓑ Ⓒ Ⓓ

6. Ⓐ Ⓑ Ⓒ Ⓓ　16. Ⓐ Ⓑ Ⓒ Ⓓ　26. Ⓐ Ⓑ Ⓒ Ⓓ

7. Ⓐ Ⓑ Ⓒ Ⓓ　17. Ⓐ Ⓑ Ⓒ Ⓓ　27. Ⓐ Ⓑ Ⓒ Ⓓ

8. Ⓐ Ⓑ Ⓒ Ⓓ　18. Ⓐ Ⓑ Ⓒ Ⓓ　28. Ⓐ Ⓑ Ⓒ Ⓓ

9. Ⓐ Ⓑ Ⓒ Ⓓ　19. Ⓐ Ⓑ Ⓒ Ⓓ　29. Ⓐ Ⓑ Ⓒ Ⓓ

10. Ⓐ Ⓑ Ⓒ Ⓓ　20. Ⓐ Ⓑ Ⓒ Ⓓ　30. Ⓐ Ⓑ Ⓒ Ⓓ

Writing Skills Answer Sheet

1. (A) (B) (C) (D)   11. (A) (B) (C) (D)   21. (A) (B) (C) (D)

2. (A) (B) (C) (D)   12. (A) (B) (C) (D)   22. (A) (B) (C) (D)

3. (A) (B) (C) (D)   13. (A) (B) (C) (D)   23. (A) (B) (C) (D)

4. (A) (B) (C) (D)   14. (A) (B) (C) (D)   24. (A) (B) (C) (D)

5. (A) (B) (C) (D)   15. (A) (B) (C) (D)   25. (A) (B) (C) (D)

6. (A) (B) (C) (D)   16. (A) (B) (C) (D)   26. (A) (B) (C) (D)

7. (A) (B) (C) (D)   17. (A) (B) (C) (D)   27. (A) (B) (C) (D)

8. (A) (B) (C) (D)   18. (A) (B) (C) (D)   28. (A) (B) (C) (D)

9. (A) (B) (C) (D)   19. (A) (B) (C) (D)   29. (A) (B) (C) (D)

10. (A) (B) (C) (D)   20. (A) (B) (C) (D)   30. (A) (B) (C) (D)

Part 1 – Reading and Language Arts

Questions 1 - 4 refer to the following passage.

The Respiratory System

The respiratory system's function is to allow oxygen exchange through all parts of the body. The anatomy or structure of the exchange system, and the uses of the exchanged gases, varies depending on the organism. In humans and other mammals, for example, the anatomical features of the respiratory system include airways, lungs, and the respiratory muscles. Molecules of oxygen and carbon dioxide are passively exchanged, by diffusion, between the gaseous external environment and the blood. This exchange process occurs in the alveolar region of the lungs.

Other animals, such as insects, have respiratory systems with very simple anatomical features, and in amphibians even the skin plays a vital role in gas exchange. Plants also have respiratory systems but the direction of gas exchange can be opposite to that of animals.

The respiratory system can also be divided into physiological, or functional, zones. These include the conducting zone (the region for gas transport from the outside atmosphere to just above the alveoli), the transitional zone, and the respiratory zone (the alveolar region where gas exchange occurs). [8]

1. What can we infer from the first paragraph in this passage?

    a. Human and mammal respiratory systems are the same.

    b. The lungs are an important part of the respiratory system.

    c. The respiratory system varies in different mammals.

    d. Oxygen and carbon dioxide are passive exchanged by the respiratory system.

2. What is the process by which molecules of oxygen and carbon dioxide are passively exchanged?

  a. Transfusion

  b. Affusion

  c. Diffusion

  d. Respiratory confusion

3. What organ plays an important role in gas exchange in amphibians?

  a. The skin

  b. The lungs

  c. The gills

  d. The mouth

4. What are the three physiological zones of the respiratory system?

  a. Conducting, transitional, respiratory zones

  b. Redacting, transitional, circulatory zones

  c. Conducting, circulatory, inhibiting zones

  d. Transitional, inhibiting, conducting zones

Questions 5 - 8 refer to the following passage.

Lightning

Lightning is an electrical discharge that occurs in a thunderstorm. Often you'll see it as a bright "bolt" (or streak) coming from the sky. Lightning occurs when static electricity inside clouds builds up and causes an electrical charge. What causes the static electricity? Water! Specifically, water droplets collide with ice crystals after the temperature in the cloud falls below freezing. Sometimes these collisions are small, but other times they're quite large. Large collisions cause large electrical charges, and when they're large enough, look out! The hyper-charged cloud will emit a burst of lightning. This lightning looks quite impressive. For a good reason, too: A lightning bolt's temperature gets so hot that it's sometimes five times hotter than the sun's surface. Although the lightning bolt is hot, it's also short-lived. Because of that, when a person is unfortunate enough to be struck by lightning, their odds of surviving are pretty good. Statistics show that 90% of victims survive a lightning blast. Oh, and that old saying, "Lightning never strikes twice in the same spot?" It's a myth! Many people report surviving lightning blasts three or more times. What's more, lightning strikes some skyscrapers multiple times. The other prominent feature of lightning storms is the thunder. This is caused by the super-heated air around a lightning bolt expands at the speed of sound. We hear thunder after seeing the lightning bolt because sound travels slower than the speed of light. In reality, though, both occur at the same moment. [9]

5. What can we infer from this passage?

a. An electrical discharge in the clouds causes lightning.

b. Lightning is not as hot as the temperature of the sun's surface.

c. The sound that lightning makes occurs when electricity strikes an object.

d. We hear lightning before we see it.

6. Being struck by lightning means:

a. Instant death.

b. Less than a fifty percent chance of survival.

c. A ninety percent chance of surviving the strike.

d. An eighty percent chance of survival.

7. Lightning is caused by the following:

a. Water droplets colliding with ice crystals creating static electricity.

b. Friction from the clouds rubbing together.

c. Water droplets colliding.

d. Warm and cold air mixing together.

Questions 9 - 12 refer to the following passage.

Low Blood Sugar

As the name suggest, low blood sugar is low sugar levels in the bloodstream. This can occur when you have not eaten properly and undertake strenuous activity, or, when you are very hungry. When Low blood sugar occurs regularly and is ongoing, it is a medical condition called hypoglycemia. This condition can occur in diabetics and in healthy adults.

Causes of low blood sugar can include excessive alcohol consumption, metabolic problems, stomach surgery, pancreas, liver or kidneys problems, as well as a side-effect of some medications.

Symptoms

There are different symptoms depending on the severity of the case.

Mild hypoglycemia can lead to feelings of nausea and hunger. The patient may also feel nervous, jittery and have fast heart beats. Sweaty skin, clammy and cold skin are likely symptoms.

Moderate hypoglycemia can result in a short temper, confusion, nervousness, fear and blurring of vision. The patient may feel weak and unsteady.

Severe cases of hypoglycemia can lead to seizures, coma, fainting spells, nightmares, headaches, excessive sweats and severe tiredness.

Diagnosis of low blood sugar

A doctor can diagnosis this medical condition by asking the patient questions and testing blood and urine samples. Home testing kits are available for patients to monitor blood sugar levels. It is important to see a qualified doctor though. The doctor can administer tests to ensure that will safely rule out other medical conditions that could affect blood sugar levels.

Treatment

Quick treatments include drinking or eating foods and drinks with high sugar contents. Good examples include soda, fruit juice, hard candy and raisins. Glucose energy tablets can also help. Doctors may also recommend medications and well as changes in diet and exercise routine to treat chronic low blood sugar.

9. Based on the article, which of the following is true?

a. Low blood sugar can happen to anyone.

b. Low blood sugar only happens to diabetics.

c. Low blood sugar can occur even.

d. None of the statements are true.

10. Which of the following are the author's opinion?

a. Quick treatments include drinking or eating foods and drinks with high sugar contents.

b. None of the statements are opinions.

c. This condition can occur in diabetics and in healthy adults.

d. There are different symptoms depending on the severity of the case

11. What is the author's purpose?

a. To inform

b. To persuade

c. To entertain

d. To analyze

12. Which of the following is not a detail?

a. A doctor can diagnosis this medical condition by asking the patient questions and testing.

b. A doctor will test blood and urine samples.

c. Glucose energy tablets can also help.

d. Home test kits monitor blood sugar levels.

Questions 13 - 16 refer to the following passage.

Myths, Legend and Folklore

Cultural historians draw a distinction between myth, legend and folktale simply as a way to group traditional stories. However, in many cultures, drawing a sharp line between myths and legends is not that simple. Instead of dividing their traditional stories into myths, legends, and folktales, some cultures divide them into two categories. The first category roughly corresponds to folktales, and the second is one that combines myths and legends. Similarly, we can not always separate myths from folktales. One society might consider a story true, making it a myth. Another society may believe the story is fiction, which makes it a folktale. In fact, when a myth loses its status as part of a religious system, it often takes on traits more typical of folktales, with its formerly divine characters now appearing as human heroes, giants, or fairies. Myth, legend, and folktale are only a few of the categories of traditional stories. Other categories include anecdotes and some kinds of jokes. Traditional stories, in turn, are only one category within the larger category of folklore, which also includes items such as gestures, costumes, and music. [10]

13. The main idea of this passage is

a. Myths, fables, and folktales are not the same thing, and each describes a specific type of story

b. Traditional stories can be categorized in different ways by different people

c. Cultures use myths for religious purposes, and when this is no longer true, the people forget and discard these myths

d. Myths can never become folk tales, because one is true, and the other is false

14. The terms myth and legend are

a. Categories that are synonymous with true and false

b. Categories that group traditional stories according to certain characteristics

c. Interchangeable, because both terms mean a story that is passed down from generation to generation

d. Meant to distinguish between a story that involves a hero and a cultural message and a story meant only to entertain

15. Traditional story categories not only include myths and legends, but

a. Can also include gestures, since some cultures passed these down before the written and spoken word

b. In addition, folklore refers to stories involving fables and fairy tales

c. These story categories can also include folk music and traditional dress

d. Traditional stories themselves are a part of the larger category of folklore, which may also include costumes, gestures, and music

16. This passage shows that

a. There is a distinct difference between a myth and a legend, although both are folktales

b. Myths are folktales, but folktales are not myths

c. Myths, legends, and folktales play an important part in tradition and the past, and are a rich and colorful part of history

d. Most cultures consider myths to be true

Questions 17 - 19 refer to the following passage.

How To Get A Good Nights Sleep

Sleep is just as essential for healthy living as water, air and food. Sleep allows the body to rest and replenish depleted energy levels. Sometimes we may for various reasons experience difficulty sleeping which has a serious effect on our health. Those who have prolonged sleeping problems are facing a serious medical condition and should see a qualified doctor when possible for help. Here is simple guide that can help you sleep better at night.

Try to create a natural pattern of waking up and sleeping around the same time everyday. This means avoiding going to bed too early and sleeping past your usual wake up time. Going to bed and getting up at radically different times everyday confuses your body clock. Try to establish a natural rhythm as much as you can.

Exercises and a bit of physical activity can help you sleep better at night. If you are having problem sleeping, try to be as active as you can during the day. If you are tired from physical activity, falling asleep is a natural and easy process for your body. If you remain inactive during the day, you will find it harder to sleep properly at night. Try walking, jogging, swimming or simple stretches as you get close to your bed time.

Afternoon naps are great to refresh you during the day, but they may also keep you awake at night. If you feel sleepy during the day, get up, take a walk and get busy to keep from sleeping. Stretching is a good way to increase blood flow to the brain and keep you alert so that you don't sleep during the day. This will help you sleep better night.

A warm bath or a glass of milk in the evening can help your body relax and prepare for sleep. A cold bath will wake you up and keep you up for several hours. Also avoid eating too late before bed.

17. How would you describe this sentence?

    a. A recommendation

    b. An opinion

    c. A fact

    d. A diagnosis

18. Which of the following is an alternative title for this article?

    a. Exercise and a good night's sleep

    b. Benefits of a good night's sleep

    c. Tips for a good night's sleep

    d. Lack of sleep is a serious medical condition

19. Which of the following can not be inferred from this article?

    a. Biking is helpful for getting a good night's sleep

    b. Mental activity is helpful for getting a good night's sleep

    c. Eating bedtime snacks is not recommended

    d. Getting up at the same time is helpful for a good night's sleep

Questions 19 - 20 refer to the following passage.

Navy SEAL

The United States Navy's Sea, Air and Land Teams, commonly known as Navy SEALs, are the U.S. Navy's principle special operations force and a part of the Naval Special Warfare Command (NSWC) as well as the maritime component of the United States Special Operations Command (USSOCOM).

The unit's acronym ("SEAL") comes from their capacity to operate at sea, in the air, and on land – but it is their ability to work underwater that separates SEALs from most other military units in the world. Navy SEALs are trained and have been deployed in a wide variety of missions, including direct action and special reconnaissance operations, unconventional warfare, foreign internal defense, hostage rescue, counter-terrorism and other missions. All SEALs are members of either the United States Navy or the United States Coast Guard.

In the early morning of 2 May 2011 local time, a team of 40 CIA-led Navy SEALs completed an operation to kill Osama bin Laden in Abbottabad, Pakistan about 35 miles (56 km) from Islamabad, the country's capital. The Navy SEALs were part of the Naval Special Warfare Development Group, previously called "Team 6." President Barack Obama later confirmed the death of bin Laden. The unprecedented media coverage raised the public profile of the SEAL community, particularly the counter-terrorism specialists commonly known as SEAL Team 6. [11]

18. Are Navy Seals part of USSOCOM?

    a. Yes.

    b. No.

    c. Only for special operations.

    d. No, they are part of the US Navy.

20. What separates Navy SEALs from other military units?

a. Belonging to NSWC.

b. Direct action and special reconnaissance operations.

c. Working underwater.

d. Working for other military units in the world.

Questions 21 - 24 refer to the following passage.

The Crusades

In 1095 Pope Urban II proclaimed the First Crusade with the intent and stated goal to restore Christian access to holy places in and around Jerusalem. Over the next 200 years there were 6 major crusades and numerous minor crusades in the fight for control of the "Holy Land." Historians are divided on the real purpose of the Crusades, some believing that it was part of a purely defensive war against Islamic conquest; some see them as part of a long-running conflict at the frontiers of Europe; and others see them as confident, aggressive, papal-led expansion attempts by Western Christendom. The impact of the crusades was profound, and judgment of the Crusaders ranges from laudatory to highly critical. However, all agree that the Crusades and wars waged during those crusades were brutal and often bloody. Several hundred thousand Roman Catholic Christians joined the Crusades, they were Christians from all over Europe.

Europe at the time was under the Feudal System, so while the Crusaders made vows to the Church they also were beholden to their Feudal Lords. This led to the Crusaders not only fighting the Saracen, the commonly used word for Muslim at the time, but also each other for power and economic gain in the Holy Land. This infighting between the Crusaders is why many historians hold the view that the Crusades were simply a front for Europe to invade the Holy Land for economic gain in the name of the Church. Another factor contributing to this theory is that while the army of crusaders marched towards Jerusalem they pillaged the land as they went. The church and feudal Lords vowing to return the land to its original beauty, and inhabitants, this rarely happened though as the Lords often kept the land for themselves. A full 800 years after the Crusades, Pope John Paul II expressed his sorrow for the massacre of innocent people and the lasting damage the Medieval church caused in that area of the World.

21. What is the tone of this article?

a. Subjective

b. Objective

c. Persuasive

d. None of the Above

22. What can all historians agree on concerning the Crusades?

a. It achieved great things

b. It stabilized the Holy Land

c. It was bloody and brutal

d. It helped defend Europe from the Byzantine Empire

23. What impact did the feudal system have on the Crusades

a. It unified the Crusaders

b. It helped gather volunteers

c. It had no effect on the Crusades

d. It led to infighting, causing more damage than good

24. What does Saracen mean?

a. Muslim

b. Christian

c. Knight

d. Holy Land

Questions 25 - 28 refer to the following two passages.

**Annabelle Lee First and Third Stanza
by Edgar Allan Poe**

It was many and many a year ago,
In a kingdom by the sea,
That a maiden there lived whom you may know
By the name of Annabel Lee;
And this maiden she lived with no other thought
Than to love and be loved by me.

But our love it was stronger by far than the love
Of those who were older than we
Of many far wiser than we
And neither the angels in heaven above,
Nor the demons down under the sea,
Can ever dissever my soul from the soul
Of the beautiful Annabel Lee.
For the moon never beams without bringing me dreams
Of the beautiful Annabel Lee;
And the stars never rise but I feel the bright eyes
Of the beautiful Annabel Lee;
And so, all the night-tide, I lie down by the side
Of my darling, my darling, my life and my bride,
In the sepulcher there by the sea,
In her tomb by the sounding sea.

Leo Tolstoy, War and Peace

"Yes, love, ...but not the love that loves for something, to
gain something, or because of something, but that love that
I felt for the first time, when dying, I saw my enemy and yet
loved him. I knew that feeling of love which is the essence
of the soul, for which no object is needed. And I know that
blissful feeling now too. To love one's neighbours; to love
one's enemies. To love everything - to Love God in all His
manifestations. Some one dear to one can be loved with human love; but an enemy can only be loved with divine love.
And that was why I felt such joy when I felt that I loved that
man. What happened to him? Is he alive? ...Loving with human love, one may pass from love to hatred; but divine love
cannot change. Nothing, not even death, can shatter it. It

is the very nature of the soul. And how many people I have hated in my life. And of all people none I have loved and hated more than her.... If it were only possible for me to see her once more... once, looking into those eyes to say..."

25. What is the difference between the two kinds of love described in these passages?

   a. One speaks to romantic love and the other Divine love

   b. There is no difference

   c. Young love, and old love

   d. Both a and c.

26. In the poem, the author refers to Annabelle Lee in the past tense, why?

   a. Because she no longer loves him

   b. Because she has died

   c. For stylistic reasons

   d. None of the above

27. Agape is Greek for "unconditional love," which passage better describes unconditional love?

   a. The Poem by Edgar Allen Poe

   b. The Excerpt from War and Peace by Leo Tolstoy

   c. Neither passage

   d. Both passages

28. The dying man in the second passage, how many people does he specifically say he loves in the passage?

   a. One

   b. Two

   c. Three

   d. Four

Questions 29 - 30 refer to the following passages.

The Daffodils
by William Wordsworth

I wandered lonely as a cloud
That floats on high o'er vales and hills,
When all at once I saw a crowd,
A host, of golden daffodils;
Beside the lake, beneath the trees,
Fluttering and dancing in the breeze.

Continuous as the stars that shine
And twinkle on the Milky Way,
They stretched in never-ending line
Along the margin of a bay:
Ten thousand saw I at a glance,
Tossing their heads in sprightly dance.

The waves beside them danced, but they
Out-did the sparkling waves in glee:
A Poet could not but be gay,
In such a jocund company:
I gazed--and gazed--but little thought
What wealth the show to me had brought:

For oft, when on my couch I lie
In vacant or in pensive mood,
They flash upon that inward eye
Which is the bliss of solitude;
And then my heart with pleasure fills,
And dances with the daffodils.

29. Is the author of this poem a lover of nature?

    a. Yes.

    b. No.

    c. Uncertain. There isn't enough information.

30. What is the general mood of this poem?

    a. Sad

    b. Thoughtful

    c. Happy

    d. Excited

Mathematics

1. The price of houses in a certain subdivision is based on the total area. Susan is watching her budget and wants to choose the house with the lowest area. Which house type, A (1300 ft²) or B, should she choose if she would like the house with the lowest price? (1cm² = 4.0ft² & π = 22/7)

    a. Type B is smaller 140 ft²

    b. Type A is smaller

    c. Type B is smaller at 855 ft²

    d. Type B is larger

2. Using the quadratic formula, solve the quadratic equation: $0.9x^2 + 1.8x - 2.7 = 0$

    a. 1 and 3

    b. -3 and 1

    c. -3 and -1

    d. -1 and 3

3. Subtract polynomials $4x^3 - 2x^2 - 10$ and $5x^3 + x^2 + x + 5$.

    a. $-x^3 - 3x^2 - x - 15$

    b. $9x^3 - 3x^2 - x - 15$

    c. $-x^3 - x^2 + x - 5$

    d. $9x^3 - x^2 + x + 5$

4. Find x and y from the following system of equations:

$(4x + 5y)/3 = ((x - 3y)/2) + 4$
$(3x + y)/2 = ((2x + 7y)/3) -1$

    a. (1, 3)

    b. (2, 1)

    c. (1, 1)

    d. (0, 1)

5. Using the factoring method, solve the quadratic equation: $x^2 + 12x - 13 = 0$

    a. -13 and 1

    b. -13 and -1

    c. 1 and 13

    d. -1 and 13

6. Using the quadratic formula, solve the quadratic equation:

$$\frac{x+2}{x-2} + \frac{x-2}{x+2} = 0$$

    a. It has infinite numbers of solutions

    b. 0 and 1

    c. It has no solutions

    d. 0

7. Turn the following expression into a simple polynomial:

$5(3x^2 - 2) - x^2(2 - 3x)$

    a. $3x^3 + 17x^2 - 10$

    b. $3x^3 + 13x^2 + 10$

    c. $-3x^3 - 13x^2 - 10$

    d. $3x^3 + 13x^2 - 10$

8. Solve $(x^3 + 2)(x^2 - x) - x^5$.

    a. $2x^5 - x^4 + 2x^2 - 2x$

    b. $-x^4 + 2x^2 - 2x$

    c. $-x^4 - 2x^2 - 2x$

    d. $-x^4 + 2x^2 + 2x$

9. $9ab^2 + 8ab^2 =$

    a. ab^2

    b. $17ab^2$

    c. 17

    d. $17a^2b^2$

10. Factor the polynomial $x^2 - 7x - 30$.

   a. $(x + 15)(x - 2)$

   b. $(x + 10)(x - 3)$

   c. $(x - 10)(x + 3)$

   d. $(x - 15)(x + 2)$

11. If a and b are real numbers, solve the following equation: $(a + 2)x - b = -2 + (a + b)x$

   a. -1

   b. 0

   c. 1

   d. 2

12. If $A = -2x^4 + x^2 - 3x$, $B = x^4 - x^3 + 5$ and $C = x^4 + 2x^3 + 4x + 5$, find A + B - C.

   a. $x^3 + x^2 + x + 10$

   b. $-3x^3 + x^2 - 7x + 10$

   c. $-2x^4 - 3x^3 + x^2 - 7x$

   d. $-3x^4 + x^3 + x^2 - 7x$

13. $(4Y^3 - 2Y^2) + (7Y^2 + 3y - y) =$

   a. $4y^3 + 9y^2 + 4y$

   b. $5y^3 + 5y^2 + 3y$

   c. $4y^3 + 7y^2 + 2y$

   d. $4y^3 + 5y^2 + 2y$

14. Turn the following expression into a simple polynomial: $1 - x(1 - x(1 - x))$

   a. $x^3 + x^2 - x + 1$

   b. $-x^3 - x^2 + x + 1$

   c. $-x^3 + x^2 - x + 1$

   d. $x^3 + x^2 - x - 1$

15. 7(2y + 8) + 1 – 4(y + 5) =

   a. $10y + 36$

   b. $10y + 77$

   c. $18y + 37$

   d. $10y + 37$

16. Richard gives 's' amount of salary to each of his 'n' employees weekly. If he has 'x' amount of money then how many days he can employ these 'n' employees.

   a. $sx/7n$

   b. $7x/nx$

   c. $nx/7s$

   d. $7x/ns$

17. Factor the polynomial $x^2 - 3x - 4$.

   a. $(x + 1)(x - 4)$

   b. $(x - 1)(x + 4)$

   c. $(x - 1)(x - 4)$

   d. $(x + 1)(x + 4)$

18. Solve the inequality:

$2x + 1/2x - 1 < 1$

   a. $(-2, + \infty)$

   b. $(1, + \infty)$

   c. $(-\infty, -2)$

   d. $(-\infty, 1/2)$

19. Using the quadratic formula, solve the quadratic equation:

$(a^2 - b^2)x^2 + 2ax + 1 = 0$

    a. $a/(a + b)$ and $b/(a + b)$

    b. $1/(a + b)$ and $a/(a + b)$

    c. $a/(a + b)$ and $a/(a - b)$

    d. $-1/(a + b)$ and $1/(a - b)$

20. Turn the following expression into a simple polynomial: $(a + b)(x + y) + (a - b)(x - y) - (ax + by)$

    a. $ax + by$

    b. $ax - by$

    c. $ax^2 + by^2$

    d. $ax^2 - by^2$

21. Given polynomials A = $4x^5 - 2x^2 + 3x - 2$ and B = $-3x^4 - 5x^2 - 4x + 5$, find A + B.

    a. $x^5 - 3x^2 - x - 3$

    b. $4x^5 - 3x^4 + 7x^2 + x + 3$

    c. $4x^5 - 3x^4 - 7x^2 - x + 3$

    d. $4x^5 - 3x^4 - 7x^2 - x - 7$

22. What is the volume of the above solid made by a hollow cylinder with half in size of the larger cylinder?

    a. 1440π in^3

    b. 1260π in^3

    c. 1040π in^3

    d. 960π in^3

23. What is the slope of the line above?

    a. -8/9

    b. 9/8

    c. -9/8

    d. 8/9

24. With the data given above, what is the value of y_1?

    a. 0
    b. -7
    c. 7
    d. 8

25. The area of a rectangle is 20 cm². If one side increases by 1 cm and other by 2 cm, the area of the new rectangle is 35 cm². Find the sides of the original rectangle.

    a. (4,8)
    b. (4,5)
    c. (2.5,8)
    d. b and c

26. What is the distance between the two points?

    a. ≈19
    b. 20
    c. ≈21
    d. ≈20

27. Find the solution for the following linear equation:
1/4 x - 2 = 5/6

    a. 0.2

    b. 0.4

    c. 0.6

    d. 0.8

28. How much water can be stored in a cylindrical container 5 meters in diameter and 12 meters high?

    a. 235.65 m³

    b. 223.65 m³

    c. 240.65 m³

    d. 252.65 m³

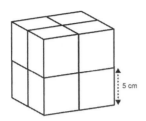

5 cm

29. What is the volume of the figure above?

    a. 125 cm³

    b. 875 cm³

    c. 1000 cm³

    d. 500 cm³

30. Solve

x √5 - y = √5
x - y √5 = 5

    a. (0, -√5)

    b. (0, √5)

    c. (-√5, 0)

    d. (√5, 0)

Writing

Directions: Choose the word or phrase that best completes the sentence.

1. _____ won first place in the Western Division?

    a. Whom

    b. Which

    c. What

    d. Who

2. **There are now several ways to listen to music, including radio, CDs, and Mp3 files _____ you can download onto an MP3 player.**

    a. on which

    b. who

    c. whom

    d. which

3. **As the tallest monument in the United States, the St. Louis Arch _____ to an impressive 630 feet.**

    a. has rose

    b. is risen

    c. rises

    d. No change is necessary.

4. **The tired, old woman should _____ on the sofa.**

    a. lie

    b. lays

    c. laid

    d. None of the options are correct.

5. Did the students understand that Thanksgiving always _____ on the fourth Thursday in November?

   a None of the options are correct.

   b. falling

   c. has fell

   d. falls

6. Collecting stamps, _____ models, and listening to shortwave radio were Rick's main hobbies.

   a. building

   b. build

   c. having built

   d. None of the options are correct.

7. Every morning, after the kids _____ for school and before the sun came up, my mother makes herself a cup of cocoa.

   a. had left

   b. leave

   c. have left

   d. None of the options are correct.

8. Elaine promised to bring the camera _____ at the mall yesterday.

   a. by me

   b. with me

   c. at me

   d. to me

9. Last night, he _____ the sleeping bag down beside my mattress.

    a. lay

    b. lain

    c. has laid

    d. laid

10. I would have bought the shirt for you if _____ you liked it.

    a. had known

    b. have known

    c. would know

    d. None of the options are correct.

11. Until you _____ the overdue books to the library, you can't take any new ones home.

    a. take

    b. bring

    c. None of the choices are correct.

12. If they had gone to the party, he would _____ too.

    a. gone

    b. went

    c. have went

    d. had went

13. His doctor suggested that he eat _____ snacks and do less lounging on the couch.

    a. less

    b. fewer

    c. None of the choices are correct.

14. His father is _____.

    a. a poet and novelist

    b. a poet and a novelist

    c. either of the above

    d. none of the above

15. Choose the sentence with the correct punctuation.

    a. George wrecked John's car that was the end of their friendship.

    b. George wrecked John's car. that was the end of their friendship.

    c. The sentence is correct.

    d. None of the choices are correct.

16. Choose the sentence with the correct punctuation.

    a. The dress was not Gina's favorite; however, she wore it to the dance.

    b. None of the choices are correct.

    c. The dress was not Gina's favorite, however; she wore it to the dance.

    d. The dress was not Gina's favorite however, she wore it to the dance.

17. Choose the sentence with the correct punctuation.

a. Chris showed his dedication to golf in many ways, for example, he watched all of the tournaments on television. .

b. The sentence is correct.

c. Chris showed his dedication to golf in many ways, for example; he watched all of the tournaments on television.

d. Chris showed his dedication to golf in many ways for example he watched all of the tournaments on television.

18. Choose the sentence with the correct grammar.

a. If Joe had told me the truth, I wouldn't have been so angry.

b. If Joe would have told me the truth, I wouldn't have been so angry.

c. I wouldn't have been so angry if Joe would have told the truth.

d. If Joe would have telled me the truth, I wouldn't have been so angry.

19. Choose the sentence with the correct punctuation.

a. I can never remember how to use those two common words, "sell," meaning to trade a product for money, or sale- meaning an event where products are traded for less money than usual.

b. I can never remember how to use those two common words, "sell," meaning to trade a product for money, or "sale," meaning an event where products are traded for less money than usual.

c. I can never remember how to use those two common words, "sell," meaning to trade a product for money, or sale, meaning an event where products are traded for less money than usual.

d. None of the above are correct.

20. Choose the sentence with the correct punctuation.

a. The class just finished reading, -"Leinengen versus the Ants," a short story by Carl Stephenson about a plantation owner's battle with army ants.

b. The class just finished reading, Leinengen versus the Ants, a short story by Carl Stephenson about a plantation owner's battle with army ants.

c. The class just finished reading, "Leinengen versus the Ants," a short story by Carl Stephenson about a plantation owner's battle with army ants.

d. None of the above

21. Choose the sentence with the correct punctuation.

a. My best friend said, "always count your change."

b. My best friend said, "Always Count your Change."

c. My best friend said, "Always count your change."

d. None of the choices are correct.

22. Choose the sentence that is written correctly.

a. He told him to rise it up

b. He told him to raise it up

c. Either of the above

d. None of the above

23. Choose the sentence that is written correctly.

a. I shall arrive early and I will have breakfast with you

b. I shall arrive early and I would have breakfast with you

c. I shall arrive early and have breakfast with you.

d. None of the above

24. Choose the sentence that is written correctly.

a. The gold coins with the diamonds is to be seized

b. The gold coins with the diamonds are to be seized.

c. None of the above

25. Choose the sentence that is written correctly.

a The trousers are to be delivered today

b. The trousers is to be delivered today.

c. Both of the above

26. Choose the sentence that is written correctly.

a. She was nodding her head, her hips are swaying.

b. She was nodding her head, her hips is swaying.

c. She was nodding her head, her hips were swaying.

d. None of the above

27. Choose the sentence that is written correctly.

a. The sad news were delivered this morning

b. The sad news are delivered this morning.

c. The sad news was delivered this morning

d. None of the above

28. Choose the sentence that is written correctly.

a. The sentence is correct

b. Mathematics are my best subject in school

c. Mathematics was my best subject in school

d. Mathematics were my best subject in school.

29. Choose the sentence that is written correctly.

a. 15 minutes is all the time you have to complete the test.

b. 15 minutes are all the time you have to complete the test.

c. Both of the above.

d. None of the above.

30. Choose the sentence that is written correctly.

a. Everyone are to wear a black tie.

b. Everyone have to wear a black tie.

c. Everyone has to wear a black tie.

d. None of the above.

Answer Key

Reading Comprehension

1. B

We can infer an important part of the respiratory system are the lungs. From the passage, "Molecules of oxygen and carbon dioxide are passively exchanged, by diffusion, between the gaseous external environment and the blood. This exchange process occurs in the alveolar region of the lungs." Therefore, one of the primary functions for the respiratory system is the exchange of oxygen and carbon dioxide, and this process occurs in the lungs. We can therefore infer that the lungs are an important part of the respiratory system.

2. C

The process by which molecules of oxygen and carbon dioxide are passively exchanged is diffusion.

This is a definition type question. Scan the passage for references to "oxygen," "carbon dioxide," or "exchanged."

3. A

The organ that plays an important role in gas exchange in amphibians is the skin.

Scan the passage for references to "amphibians," and find the answer.

4. A

The three physiological zones of the respiratory system are Conducting, transitional, respiratory zones.

5. A

We can infer that, an electrical discharge in the clouds causes lightning.

The passage tells us that, "Lightning occurs when static electricity inside clouds builds up and causes an electrical charge,"

6. C

Being struck by lightning means, a ninety percent chance of

surviving the strike.

From the passage, "statistics show that 90% of victims survive a lightning blast."

7. A
We know that lightning is static electricity from the third sentence in the passage. We also know that water droplets colliding with ice crystals cause static electricity. Therefore, Lightning is caused by water droplets colliding with ice crystals.

8. A
Low blood sugar occurs both in diabetics and healthy adults.

9. B
None of the statements are the author's opinion.

10. A
The author's purpose is the inform.

11. A
The only statement that is not a detail is, "A doctor can diagnosis this medical condition by asking the patient questions and testing."

12. B
This passage describes the different categories for traditional stories. The other choices are facts from the passage, not the main idea of the passage. The main idea of a passage will always be the most general statement. For example, choice A, Myths, fables, and folktales are not the same thing, and each describes a specific type of story. This is a true statement from the passage, but not the main idea of the passage, since the passage also talks about how some cultures may classify a story as a myth and others as a folktale. The statement, from choice B, Traditional stories can be categorized in different ways by different people, is a more general statement that describes the passage.

13. B
Choice B is the best choice, categories that group traditional stories according to certain characteristics.

Choices A and C are false and can be eliminated right away. Choice D is designed to confuse. Choice D may be true, but it is not mentioned in the passage.

14. D
The best answer is D, traditional stories themselves are a part of the larger category of folklore, which may also include costumes, gestures, and music.

All the other choices are false. Traditional stories are part of the larger category of Folklore, which includes other things, not the other way around.

15. A
The sentence is a recommendation.

16. C
Tips for a good night's sleep is the best alternative title for this article.

17. B
Mental activity is helpful for a good night's sleep is can not be inferred from this article.

18. C
This question tests the reader's vocabulary and contextualization skills. Choice A may or may not be true, but focuses on the wrong function of the word "give" and ignores the rest of the sentence, which is more relevant to what the passage is discussing. Choices B and D may also be selected if the reader depends too literally on the word "give," failing to grasp the more abstract function of the word that is the focus of choice C, which also properly acknowledges the entirety of the passage and its meaning.

19. A
Navy Seals are the maritime component of the United States Special Operations Command (USSOCOM).

20. C
Working underwater separates SEALs from other military units. This is taken directly from the passage.

21. A

Choice B is incorrect; the author did not express their opinion on the subject matter. Choice C is incorrect, the author was not trying to prove a point.

22. C

Choice C is correct; historians believe it was brutal and bloody. Choice A is incorrect; there is no consensus that the Crusades achieved great things. Choice B is incorrect; it did not stabilize the Holy Lands. Choice D is incorrect, some historians do believe this was the purpose but not all historians.

23. D

The feudal system led to infighting. Choice A is incorrect, it had the opposite effect. Choice B is incorrect, though this is a good answer, it is not the best answer. The Church asked for volunteers not the Feudal Lords. Choice C is incorrect, it did have an effect on the Crusades.

24. A

Saracen was a generic term for Muslims widely used in Europe during the later medieval era.

25. A

The first speaks to romantic love, a boy has for Annabelle Lee, the second divine love. Choice B is incorrect for the same reason - both passages speak of different types of love. Choice C is incorrect. While the first passage alludes to young love the second passage makes no distinction.

26. B

A careful reading will show in the last line, she is in a tomb, meaning she has died. Choice A is incorrect. While this could be correct, it is not the best and most accurate answer, because she has died. Choice C is incorrect because the past tense is used for a specific reason and has nothing to do with style.

27. B

Divine love is unchanging and therefore unconditional. Choice A is incorrect since romantic love can be conditional. Choice C is incorrect, the second passage is correct. Choice D is incorrect, the first passage is incorrect.

28. C

He loves three people, the man, his enemy, and the un-named woman.

29. A

The author is enjoying the daffodils very much, so we can infer that he is a lover of nature.

30. C

The mood of this poem is happy.   From the last line,

And then my heart with pleasure fills,
And dances with the daffodils.

Mathematics

1. C

Area of Type B = $[(12 \times 8) + (14 \times 8) + (1/2 \times 22/7 \times 7^2)]$
96 + 112 + 77
285 m^2
Converting to feet = 3 x 285 ft^2
Area of Type B = 855 ft^2

2. B

$0.9x^2 + 1.8x - 2.7 = 0$ * 10

$9x^2 + 18x - 27 = 0 \div 9$
$x^2 + 2x - 3 = 0$

$x_{1,2} = -2 \pm \sqrt{2^2} - 4 * (-3)/2$
$x_{1,2} = -2 \pm \sqrt{4} + 12/2$
$x_{1,2} = -2 \pm \sqrt{16}/2$
$x_{1,2} = -2 \pm 4$
$x_1 = -2 + 4/2 = 1$
$x_2 = -2 - 4/2 = -3$

3. A

$(4x^3 - 2x^2 - 10) - (5x^3 + x^2 + x + 5)$
$4x^3 - 2x^2 - 10 - 5x^3 - x^2 - x - 5$
$-x^3 - 3x^2 - x - 15$

4. C
Divide both equations by 6, for,

2(4x + 5y) = 3(x - 3y) + 24
3(3x + 7) = 2(2x + 7y) - 6

8x + 10y = 3x - 9y + 24
9x + 3y = 4x + 14y = 6

8x + 10y = 3x - 9y + 24
9x + 3y = 4x + 14y - 6

5x + 19y = 24
5x = 11y = -6

5x + 19y - (5x - 11y) = 24 - (-6)
5x + 19y - 5x + 11y = 24 + 6

30y = 30
y = 1

5x + 19y = 24

5x + 19 = 24

5x = 24 - 19 = 5

x = 1

5. A
-13 and 1
$x^2 + 12x - 13$
$x^2 + 13x - x - 13 = 0$
$x(x + 13) - (x + 13) = 0$
$(x + 13)(x - 1) = 0$
X = -13   X = 1

6. C
This equation has no solution.

$x^2 + 4x + 4 + x^2 - 4x + 4$ / $(x - 2)(x + 2) = 0$

$2x^2 + 8$ / $(x - 2)(x + 2) = 0 => 2x^2 + 8 = 0$
$x^2 + 4 = 0$
$x_{1,2} = 0 \pm \sqrt{-4 * 4}$ / 2

$x_{1,2} = 0 \pm \sqrt{-16} / 2$
Solution for the square root of -16 is not a real number, so this equation has no solution.

7. D
$3x^3 + 13x^2 - 10$
$5(3x^2 - 2) - x^2(2 - 3x)$
$15x^2 - 10 - 2x^2 + 3x^3$
$3x^3 + 13x^2 - 10$

8. B
$-x^4 + 2x^2 - 2x$
$(x^3 + 2)(x^2 - x) - x^5$
$x^5 - x^4 + 2x^2 - 2x - x^5$
$-x^4 + 2x^2 - 2x$

9. B
$ab^2(9 + 8) = 17ab^2$

10. C
$x^2 - 7x - 30 = x * x - 10x + 3x - 3 * 10 = x(x - 10) + 3(x - 10) = (x - 10)(x + 3)$

11. A
$(a + 2)x - b = -2 + (a + b)x$
$ax + 2x - b = -2 + ax + bx$
$ax + 2x - ax - bx = -2 + b$
$2x - bx = -2 + b$
$(2 - b)x = -(2 - b)$
$x = -(2 - b) : (2 - b)$
$x = -1$

12. C
$-2x^4 - 3x^3 + x^2 - 7x$
$A + B - C = (-2x^4 + x^2 - 3x) + (x^4 - x^3 + 5) - (x^4 + 2x^3 + 4x + 5)$
$-2x^4 + x^2 - 3x + x^4 - x^3 + 5 - x^4 - 2x^3 - 4x - 5$
$-2x^4 - 3x^3 + x^2 - 7x$

13. D
Remove parenthesis
$4Y^3 - 2Y^2 + 7Y^2 + 3Y - Y =$
add and subtract like terms, $4Y^3 + 5Y^2 + 2Y$

14. C

$1 - x(1 - x(1 - x))$

$1 - x(1 - x + x^2)$

$1 - x + x^2 - x^3$

$-x^3 + x^2 - x + 1$

15. D

Open parenthesis, $(7 \times 2y + 7 \times 8) + 1- (4 \times y -20) =$

$14y + 56 + 1 - 4y - 20,$

Collect like terms $=14y -4y + 56 + 1 - 20 = 10y + 37$

16. D

He pays 'ns' amount to the employees for 7 days. The 'x' amount will be for '7x/ns' days.

17. A

$x^2 - 3x - 4 = x * x + x - 4x - 4 = x(x + 1) - 4(x + 1) = (x + 1)(x - 4)$

18. D

$(2x + 1 / 2x - 1) < 1$

$(2x + 1 / 2x - 1) - 1 < 0$

$(2x + 1 - 2x + 1 / 2x - 1) < 0$

$2 / 2x - 1 < 0$

2 is a positive number, so

$2x - 1 < 0$

$2x < 1$

$x < 1/2$

19. D

$$-\frac{1}{a+b} \text{ and } -\frac{1}{a-b}$$

$$(a^2 - b^2)x^2 + 2ax + 1 = 0$$

$$x_{1,2} = \frac{-2a \pm \sqrt{(2a)^2 - 4(a^2 - b^2)}}{2(a^2 - b^2)}$$

$$x_{1,2} = \frac{-2a \pm \sqrt{4a^2 - 4a^2 + 4b^2}}{2(a^2 - b^2)}$$

$$x_{1,2} = \frac{-2a \pm \sqrt{4b^2}}{2(a^2 - b^2)}$$

$$x_{1,2} = \frac{-2a \pm 2b}{2(a^2 - b^2)}$$

$$x_{1,2} = \frac{-a \pm b}{a^2 - b^2} = \frac{-a \pm b}{(a-b)(a+b)}$$

$$x_1 = \frac{-a + b}{(a-b)(a+b)} = \frac{-(a-b)}{(a-b)(a+b)} = -\frac{1}{(a+b)}$$

$$x_2 = \frac{-a - b}{(a-b)(a+b)} = \frac{-(a+b)}{(a-b)(a+b)} = -\frac{1}{(a-b)}$$

20. A

$(a + b) (x + y) + (a - b) (x - y) - (ax + by)$
$= ax + ay + bx + by + ax - ay - bx + by - ax - by$
$ax + by$

21. C

$4x^5 - 3x^4 - 7x^2 - x + 3$
$A + B = (4x^5 - 2x^2 + 3x - 2) + (-3x^4 - 5x^2 - 4x + 5) =$
$4x^5 - 2x^2 + 3x - 2 - 3x^4 - 5x^2 - 4x + 5$
$4x^5 - 3x^4 - 7x^2 - x + 3$

22. B

Total Volume = Volume of large cylinder - Volume of small cylinder
Volume of cylinder = area of base x height
Volume= $(\pi 12^2 x 10) - (\pi 6^2 x 5)$, $1440\pi - 180\pi$
Volume= 1260π in^3

23. A

Slope (m) = $\frac{\text{change in y}}{\text{change in x}}$

$(x_1, y_1) = (-9,6)$ & $(x_2, y_2) = (18,-18)$
Slope = $(-18 - 6)/[18-(-9)] = -24/27 = -8/9$

24. A

$x_1, = -4$, $(x_2, y_2) = (-8,7)$ & slope = $-7/4$
$(7 - y_1)/[-8-(-4)] = -7/4$
$(7 - y_1)/-4 = -7/4$
$7 - y_1 = 7$
$y_1 = 0$

25. D

$ab = 20 => a = 20/b$
$(a + 1) (b + 2) = 35$

$(20/b + 1) (b + 2) = 35$
$20 + 40/b + b + 2 = 35$
$20b + 40 + b^2 = 33b$
$b^2 - 13b + 40 = 0$
$b_{1,2} = 13 \pm \sqrt{169 - 160} / 2$
$b_{1,2} = 13 \pm 3 / 2$
$b_1 = 8$
$b_2 = 5$

$a_1 = 20/b_1 = 20/8 = 2.5$
$a_2 = 20/b_2 = 20/5 = 4$

26. D
Distance between 2 points = $[(x_2 - x_1)^2 + (y_2 - y_1)^2]^{1/2}$

Distance = $[(18 - 9)^2 + (12 + 6)^2]^{1/2}$
Distance = $[(9)^2 + (18)^2]^{1/2}$
Distance = $(81 + 324)^{1/2}$
Distance = $(405)^{1/2}$
Since $20^2 = 400$ & $21^2 = 441$, $19^2 = 361$ therefore the distance is about 20.

27. D
$1/4x - 2 = 5/6$
$1 = 5 (4x - 2)/6$
$6 = 5(4x - 2)$
$6 = 20x - 10$
$-20x = -10 - -6$
$-20x = -16$
$x = -16/-20 = 0.8$

28. B
The formula of the volume of cylinder is = $\sqcap$ r^2h. Where $\sqcap$ is 3.142, r is radius of the cross sectional area, and h is the height. So the volume will be = $3.142 \times 2.5^2 \times 12 = 235.65$ m^3.

29. C
Large cube is made up of 8 smaller cubes of 5 cm sides.
Volume = Volume of small cube x 8
Volume = (5 x 5 x 5) x 8, 125 x 8
Volume = 1000 cm^3

30. A
$(0, -\sqrt{5})$

$y = x\sqrt{5} - \sqrt{5}$
$x - (x\sqrt{5} - \sqrt{5}) \sqrt{5} = 5$
$x - 5x + 5 = 5$
$-4x = 5 - 5$
$-4x = 0$

$$y = x\sqrt{5} - \sqrt{5}$$
$$y = 0\sqrt{5} - \sqrt{5}$$
$$y = \sqrt{5}$$

Remove the brackets, but change all signs in the third polynomial because of the minus sign. Now group the variables by degrees.

Writing

1. D
"Who" is correct because the question uses an active construction. "To whom was first place given?" is passive construction.

2. D
"Which" is correct, because the files are objects and not people.

3. C
The simple present tense, "rises," is correct.

4. A
"Lie" does not require a direct object, while "lay" does. The old woman might lie on the couch, which has no direct object, or she might lay the book down, which has the direct object, "the book."

5. D
The simple present tense, "falls," is correct because it is repeated action.

6. A
The present progressive, "building models," is correct in this sentence; it is required to match the other present progressive verbs.

7. C
Past Perfect tense describes a completed action in the past, before another action in the past.

8. D
The preposition "to" is the correct preposition to use with "bring."

9. D
"Laid" is the past tense.

10. A
This is a past unreal conditional sentence. It requires an 'if' clause and a result clause, and either clause can appear first. The 'if' clause uses the past perfect, while the result clause uses the past participle.

11. C
Bring vs. Take. Usage depends on your location. Something coming your way is brought to you. Something going away is taken from you.

12. A
The sentence is correct. Went vs. Gone. Went is the simple past tense. Gone is used in the past perfect.

13. B
Fewer vs. Less. 'Fewer' is used with countables and 'less' is used with uncountables.

14. B
His father is a poet and a novelist. It is necessary to use 'a' twice in this sentence for the two distinct things.

15. C
The semicolon links independent clauses. An independent clause can form a complete sentence by itself.

16. A
The semicolon links independent clauses with a conjunction (However).

17. B
The sentence is correct. The semicolon links independent clauses. An independent clause can form a complete sentence by itself.

18. A

The third conditional is used for talking about an unreal situation (that did not happen) in the past. For example, "If I had studied harder, [if clause] I would have passed the exam [main clause]. Which is the same as, "I failed the exam, because I didn't study hard enough."

19. B

Here the word "sale" is used as a "word" and not as a word in the sentence, so quotation marks are used.

20. C

Titles of short stories are enclosed in quotation marks, and commas always go inside quotation marks.

21. A

Quoted speech is not capitalized.

22. B

The verb raise ('to increase', 'to lift up.') can appear in three forms, raise, raised and raised.

23. C

The two verbs "shall" and "will" should not be used in the same sentence when referring to the same future.

24. B

When two subjects are linked with "with" or "as well," use the verb form that matches the first subject.

25. A

Use a plural verb for nouns like measles, tongs, trousers, riches, scissors etc.

26. C

A verb can fit any of the two subjects in a compound sentence since the verb form agrees with that subject.

27. C

Always use the singular verb form for nouns like politics, wages, mathematics, innings, news, advice, summons, furniture, information, poetry, machinery, vacation, scenery etc.

28. C

Always use the singular verb form for nouns like politics,

wages, mathematics, innings, news, advice, summons, furniture, information, poetry, machinery, vacation, scenery etc.

29. A
Use a singular verb with a plural noun that refers to a specific amount or quantity that is considered as a whole (dozen, hundred score etc).

30. C
Use a singular verb with either, each, neither, everyone and many.

Conclusion

CONGRATULATIONS! You have made it this far because you have applied yourself diligently to practicing for the exam and no doubt improved your potential score considerably! Getting into a good school is a huge step in a journey that might be challenging at times but will be many times more rewarding and fulfilling. That is why being prepared is so important.

Good Luck!

FREE Ebook Version

Download a FREE Ebook version of the publication!

Suitable for tablets, iPad, iPhone, or any smart phone.

Go to
http://www.tinyurl.com/pogt431

Register for Free Updates and More Practice Test Questions

Register your purchase at www.test-preparation.ca/register.html for fast and convenient access to updates, errata, free test tips and more practice test questions.

PERT Test Strategy!

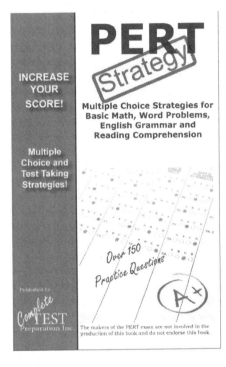

PERT ~~Strategy~~

INCREASE YOUR SCORE!

Multiple Choice Strategies for Basic Math, Word Problems, English Grammar and Reading Comprehension

Multiple Choice and Test Taking Strategies!

Over 150 Practice Questions

A+

Published by

Complete TEST Preparation Inc.

The makers of the PERT exam are not involved in the production of this book and do not endorse this book.

Learn to increase your score using time-tested secrets for answering multiple choice questions!

This practice book has everything you need to know about answering multiple choice questions on a standardized test!

You will learn 12 strategies for answering multiple choice questions and then practice each strategy with over 45 reading comprehension multiple choice questions, with extensive commentary from exam experts!

Maybe you have read this kind of thing before, and maybe feel you don't need it, and you are not sure if you are going to buy this Book.

Remember though, it only a few percentage points divide the PASS from the FAIL students.

Even if our multiple choice strategies increase your score by a few percentage points, isn't that worth it?

Go to

https://www.createspace.com/4610546

Enter Code LYFZGQB5 for 25% off!

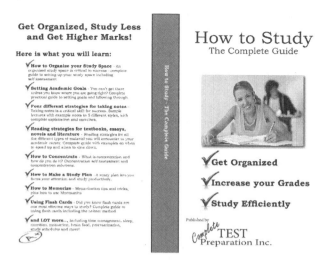

Endnotes

Reading Comprehension passages where noted below are used under the Creative Commons Attribution-ShareAlike 3.0 License

http://en.wikipedia.org/wiki/Wikipedia:Text_of_Creative_Commons_Attribution-ShareAlike_3.0_Unported_License

[1] Immune System. In *Wikipedia*. Retrieved November 12, 2010 from, en.wikipedia.org/wiki/Immune_system.

[2] White Blood Cell. In *Wikipedia*. Retrieved November 12, 2010 from en.wikipedia.org/wiki/White_blood_cell.

[3] Infectious disease. In *Wikipedia*. Retrieved November 12, 2010 from http://en.wikipedia.org/wiki/Infectious_disease.

[4] Thunderstorm. In *Wikipedia*. Retrieved November 12, 2010 from en.wikipedia.org/wiki/Thunderstorm.

[5] Meteorology. In *Wikipedia*. Retrieved November 12, 2010 from en.wikipedia.org/wiki/Outline_of_meteorology.

[6] Cloud. In *Wikipedia*. Retrieved November 12, 2010 from http://en.wikipedia.org/wiki/Clouds.

[7] Mary Shelley, Frankenstein, In Gutenberg. Retrieved October 13, 2014 http://www.gutenberg.org/files/84/84-h/84-h.htm

[8] Respiratory System. In *Wikipedia*. Retrieved November 12, 2010 from en.wikipedia.org/wiki/Respiratory_system.

[9] Lightning. In *Wikipedia*. Retrieved November 12, 2010 from http://en.wikipedia.org/wiki/Lightning.

[10] Mythology. In *Wikipedia*. Retrieved November 12, 2010 from en.wikipedia.org/wiki/Mythology.

[11] U.S. Navy Seal. In *Wikipedia*. Retrieved November 12, 2010 from en.wikipedia.org/wiki/United_States_Navy_SEALs.